Andros Island, Travel Guide, and Environmental Information

History, Vacation, Holiday, Environment

Author

Michael Thomson

. Copyright Notice

Table of Content

Introduction

About Andros

Andros is an island that has enough tourism to be quite well organised, but not so much that it has become too commercialised.

A fairly green island for the Cyclades, Andros offers some really nice beaches, pretty villages and a quiet, relaxed atmosphere. It is the second largest island among the Cyclades, and its high mountains and deep valleys make an unforgettable impression.

Although not a party island, the nightlife here is quite varied and those who love fishing, sailing and snorkelling will certainly find their paradise

Geography: Andros is the most northerly and second largest island of the Cyclades after Naxos. Its size is 374 square kilometres, with a length of 39.8 kilometres and a width of 16.7 kilometres at its widest. There is approximately 110 kilometres of coastline. The terrain is mountainous but the habited areas are relatively level. The island is divided into five regions by four mountainous masses. These are, Mount Saranda (725 metres) which faces north from the highlands of Makrotandalos (approx height 200 metres) and south from the valleys of Batsi, Ateni and Katakoilos.

Mount Petalo the main mountain on the island, with the highest peak of Andros (Kouvara at 994 metres) lies between the above mentioned valleys to the north and the valley of Messaria in the south. Mount Gerakonas (at 720 metres) lies between the valleys of Messaria and Korthi.

Finally, is Mount Pachi (at 681 metres) which is south of the valley of Korthi and ends at the most southern tip of the island.

Four small rivers cross the island from west to east.These rivers, along with the mountains, are the beauties of Andros. Unlike many Greek islands they flow all year round fed by the mountain peaks. The River Arnipotamos flows into the bay of Lefka, the River Achla which flows into the bay of Achla, the Megalos Potamos River flows into Paraporti beach in Hora and the Dipotamata River flows into the bay of Syneti. Aside from these rivers there are around seven streams which also flow continuously all year.

This makes a total of eleven waterways, nearly all of which shape small aquatic areas at the mouths, with rich vegetation and remarkable aquatic fauna.

The coastline of Andros is particularly rugged creating many small, picturesque bays, which mostly have good sandy beaches. Some of the largest bays on the island which are worth mentioning are Gavrio, Batsi, Hora and Korthion, all of which have organised harbours, Also is the bay of Fourni and in the north is the beach of Agios Petros, which is mentioned by Lloyds as a safe haven for boats.

Andros is completely different to all other islands in the Cyclades. With its high and craggy mountains, deep, green and fertile valleys, its abundant running water, plateaus, terraced farmlands, steep coasts and the many large and small golden sandy beaches, is one of constant contrasts and surprises. Its perfect for gentle strolling, hiking or driving and within a few kilometres the landscape surroundings change dramatically.

One moment you are in a dry, scrubby windswept area and the next in a forest of pines, or a wood of chestnut, plane and oak trees with the sound of running water babbling over its stony riverbed. You can move from the sunbaked sandy beach with clear sparkling blue sea of the seashore to green and fertile valley or lush gorge that is rich with vegetation and flora.

Agriculture on Andros is plentiful although the areas for cultivation are relatively small due to being confined to the valley areas that lie between the mountains, tucked in snugly to

protect them from the strong winds that are characteristic of all the Cycladic islands. The plentiful water and vegetation of the area has made the soild particularly good making the valleys exceptionally fertile and bountiful.

History According to mythology, Andros was a grandson of Apollo and general under the Cretan king Rhadamanthus. Because he had served the king well, he was given this island.

Many peoples have lived on Andros: it was first settled by Carians, Phoenicians and Cretans in the 2nd millennium BC. Much later, in the 5th century BC, it was conquered by Persia, and so joined the Athenian league for protection. Athens demanded too high tributes, though, and so Andros changed sides and joined the Spartans.

In the 4th century the island was ruled by the Macedonians, and then by the Romans.

The Venetians ruled Andros from the beginning of the 13th century, and by then the island was very rich. The Byzantine years had been good to it, and because of the defense, it had managed to ward off most pirate attacks.

The Turks invaded in 1537 under general Barbarossa. Andros fought hard in the war of Independence that broke out in 1821, and was liberated nine years later.

The greatest catastrophe came in 1943 when the Germans bombarded the island until it was completely destroyed. Read more about the History of Andros

What to See in Andros' capital, Chora, there is a museum about the island's shipbuilding through times. There is also an archaeological museum with artefacts from many periods in history.

The Sariza wells are natural wells where you can drink that water straight out of them. Much of the bottled water on Andros comes from here.

Menites is a lovely village to stroll around in. The tree covered valley of Messaria covers the complete width of Andros from the west to the east and ends at the coastal capital town of Hora. Here you can find some of the most beautiful villages of the island. On the northeren side are the villages of Strapouries, Pitrofos, Menites, Lamira, Mesathouri and Ipsilou and, to the south the villages of Aladino, Falika, Koureli and Sasa.

In Byzantine times, all this area, with Messaria at its centre, was the epicentre for the economic development of Andros. The same area saw a second boost in its

development at the beginning of the 20th Century with the growth of navigation. In this area, too, you will find many of the island's beautiful Byzantine churches and the Monastery of Panayia Panachrantou (Virgin Mary). Hora itself, stands out as an elegant and well-maintained town. Here you can see the beautiful, neo-classical town houses and mansions of the upper-classes and ships' captains who lived here throughout the last century. All of these features pigeon house androsare found in a lush, idyllic landscape of gardens and rich farmlands, which owe their existence to the plentiful water, which literally flows everywhere. The final wonderful quality of Hora is its peace and tranquillity owing to the fact that its main centre is pedestrianised.

Cars are parked at the edge of the centre and the centre itself is reached by foot. The same goes for the outlying villages. You can only go as far as the outskirts of each village by car

and from there on walking using the village lanes. Furthermore, the whole island is a paradise for walkers as you can visit all this, taking in a complete picture of the area, by means of a large and well maintained network of footpaths.

Gavrio is where all visitors enter the island and, although there is no known historical background to this town, it lseems it was an ancient port that connected Andros to Attica in the same way it does today. As the ship enters the port you can see the small town of Gavrio which has many kinds of shops, cafes, restaurants and tavernas on the seafront. Walking along the promenade you can find small sandy beaches. From Gavrio, buses depart to Hora. If you want to discover Andros under your own steam, you will find car hire firms and tourist offices at the portside.

Also, if you are interested to buy land or property on Andros, here you will find many real estate agencies. A good idea is to visit Ano Gavrio, either by foot or car. The road takes you through glorious countryside and farmland, over babbling brooks and passes a fine example of the famed pigeon houses of Andros, the pigeon house of Manjoros is just past the first little bridge over a river and is easy to spot with its traditional quaint structure and decoration. Continuing along this road will lead you to the church of Agia Sofia, the main church of Gavrio.

Batsi: Next to Gavrio, towards Batsi, is the wonderful sandy beach of Agios Petros. Here is located the interesting Tower of Agios Petros which is worth a closer look. Batsi is probably the most developed tourist town of the island, although it must be said that it is nothing like the mass tourist developments that can be seen on other Cycladic islands. At Batsi you will find most of the hotels, apartments and the only camping site on the island. Batsi has a small marina where yachts and fishing boats berth. Around the marina and along the promenade you will find many restaurants, tavernas and clubs. Batsi, like Gavrio, belongs to the municipality of Hydrousa. The most beaches of Andros can be found here as well as many picturesque villages clustered on the slopes of the mountains and the bays.

What to Do : Andros is a perfect island not only for walkers but also for people who like to swim, snorkel, fish and sail. Every summer sailing races are organised and there are countless wonderful beaches for windsurfing on the island fuelled by the well-known Cycladic winds. At the little harbour town of Batsi there are various water sports available during the summer season. Recently the Town Council of Andros has developed a programme to develop and support low-key tourism.

This has involved clearing and signposting the basic network of footpaths on the island for the use of residents and visitors alike. Although the maintenance of these fishing-in-androspaths is at times patchy, they do provide an ideal way of getting around the island.

If you want to experience the history and tradition of over six thousand years in Andros and to get to know its wonderful and special nature, its mineral and curative waters, its fauna and its hundreds of species of wild flowers and herbs (some of which can only be found here in Andros),- then all you need to do is follow the ancient paths which have supported the socioeconomic life of the island from prehistoric times until the early post-war years. The experience will be one that will stay with you forever.

Beaches The most popular beach is probably Batsi, but other places to recommend are also Agios Petros, Fellos, Korthi, Gavrio, Kypri, Lefka, Kaminaki.and the bay of Korthi.

Nighttlife: If you insist on "clubbing" a bit, there are music bars in Batsi and Gavrion, at least during high season. There are also many bars, and you can enjoy both Greek and foreign music, whatever you prefer. In Chora there is also an outdoor cinema: all films are shown in their original languages with Greek subtitles.

Food There are many taverns and restaurants on Andros, and quite a few local specialities. You should try the local sausages, sun dried wine and various mezedakia - tit bits. The pastries should not be missed: Andros is renowned for its excellent sweets especially those that are made of almonds the famous "kaltsounia". Coming out of the ferry in Gavrio the restaurant 'Konaki' right on the waterfront offers excellent Greek cuisine. In Chora you will find local meze dishes in 'Nefeli' opposite the church of Panagia, in Georgiou Empeirikou street that leads to the Archaeological museum in Korai square and further down to the Maritime Museum and the statue of the Unknown Sailor.

Shopping: There are many shops in Andros town, Chora, as well as in Batsi. Apart from the usual souvenirs, you can also get textiles, jewelry and ceramics.

Getting Around Andros is quite a large island, so it is definitely a good idea to rent a vehicle. There are also local buses connecting some of the main villages, as well as taxis. From Gavrion the buses to Chora are at the exit of the port.

Getting There: There is no airport on Andros, so you'll have to fly to Athens or maybe Mykonosand take the boat from there. The suggested itinerary is from

Athens (Rafina) , there are daily 3-4 ferries departing from Rafina to Andros check here for the daily departures. The orange buses (KTEL) for Rafina depart from Pedion Areos (ticket price 2.10 euro). A faster option is to take the Athens Metro until the station 'Ethniki Amyna' in Mesogeion street and from there to continue with the KTEL bus to the port of Rafina.

History

About the history of Andros island, Greece

Prehistoric period

The rich history of Andros can be traced back to antiquity where the island was known as Gavros. It was also called Hydroussa, Epagris and Lasia, based on poetic designations referring to the abundant waters and rich vegetation of the Island. Archaeological excavations and the finding of remains of developed settlements have proved that the island was inhabited during the Mycenaean times or even earlier. Its earliest inhabitants are supposed to have been Carians,

Pelasgians, Phoenicians, Cretans, while in 1000 BC, Andros got colonized by the Ionians.

During the Geometric period (9th-7th centuries BC), the island became historically recognised. Traces of a Geometric settlement have been found in the village of Zagora, at the south-western side of the island. A considerable part of the old town has been unearthed as well as private dwellings, a sanctuary, a temple, a fortification wall that have a gate built with similar techniques to those used on the Lion gate in Mycenae.

The second half of the 8th century BC was the period of the island's greatest prosperity. During the 7th century BC, Andros participated with the Halkideans to the colonization of Halkidiki as well as the coastal areas of Trace Northern Greece. Up to the 6th century BC, Andros became an independent city-state belonging to the ancient Amphictyony of Delos. The god of wine and festivities, Dionysus, was worshiped as patron of the island. The inhabitants spoke the Ionian dialect.

Ancient times

During the Classical times, the capital of Andros was Paleopolis, whose prosperity is proved by the discovery of 60 silver and bronze coins of the Andriot state as well as by the sunken remains of an ancient agora (market) and the remains of the western part of the wall surrounding the capital. During the Persian Wars, Andros went under Persian domination until the naval Battle of Salamis (480 BC). Then it fell under Athenian domination, paying taxes and forced to send men to fight in the Peloponnesian War. After the war, Andros stayed under the dominance of Sparta, the winner of the war, and was liberated by the Athenians in 393 BC. Later on the island participated and distinguished itself in the battle of Chaeroneia, in 338 BC.

After the battle of Chaeroneia, the island of Andros came under the rule of Philip the Macedonian and afterwards under his son's rule, Alexander the Great.

Andros stayed under Macedonian domination until 315 BC. The successors of Alexander the Great were hostile one to another and could not come to a fair separation of the lands, which leaded to a successive conquest of the island by some Egyptian and Macedonian kings. The situation resulted in important changes in the political system, cults and customs. Andros followed the same fate as the other Aegean islands and continental Greece, consecutively falling under Roman, Venetian and Ottoman domination.

Byzantine times

Andros fell under the Roman rule in 129 BC. Pirates and civil wars between Roman governors made the inhabitants of Andros suffer from poverty, while they were badly maltreated. With the years of Emperor Hadrian, their fate became a little better. In the early Byzantine times, the island became property of a Byzantine drungarius (military rank) of the Aegean Sea.

Many Byzantine churches and monasteries have been preserved since that period.

Venetian times

Constantinople fell to the Crusaders in 1204 AD and Andros came under the rule of Marino Dandolo, a direct emissary from Venice. Three years later, Dandolo recognised the sovereignty of the duke of Naxos, Marco Sanudo. Later, the Sanudo family took the power and the rule of the island until 1384, when Petro Zeno was brought as the ruler of Andros by Francesco Crispo. This new leader was the most effective one, bringing security, financial and demographic strength to the island.

In the middle of the 15th century, the Somaripa family of Paros took the island, but the inhabitants chased them because of the great oppression they exercised on the island. They created a provisional government which came directly under Turkish rule in 1579. The

Venetians leaders laid the foundations of feudalism on the island, which influenced the society of Andros for a long time. They built mansions and castles, such as Faneromeni Castle, and at this time, the basis for the prosperity in the area was the silkworm trade.

Ottoman occupation

The inhabitants of Andros had more privileges than other islands. The Turkish authorities were forbidden of treating badly the islanders or of forcing them to convert to Islam. Some taxes were abolished and property titles or contracts were recognised by the rulers. The inhabitants could wear their local costumes, follow their religion and preserve their churches and monasteries. Of course, the head tax and other taxes as well as some violations of the privileges still existed, but the occupation of the locals with trade brought much income to the Ottoman Empire. At the church of Agia Triada, in Korthi, a school was founded in 1813 by the monk Samuel Plasimis, a little before the Greek War of Independence.

Recent years

Before the Greek Revolution of 1821, 37 Andriots were members of the Society of Friends, a secret society working against the Ottoman rule and from which most members were coming from the Greek islands. Theofilos Kairis proclaimed officially the War of Independence on the 10th of May 1821, raising the flag of the Revolution in the church of Agios Georgios in Chora. The period following the Revolution was also when Andros entered in a great economic prosperity by its superiority in shipping. Its inhabitants were living in great prosperity and wealth.

During 1923 and 1930, Andros was only second to Piraeus regarding ship registration, and the second port of Greece. But World War II caused great losses in human lives and ships, as well as the period of the

Italian and the German occupation, during which Hora was bombed and some of the most beautiful mansions of Andros were destroyed. Mass migration was a characteristic of the modern times in Andros.

In the 19th century, a lot of the inhabitants moved to cosmopolitan centres, like Constantinople, Smyrna, Alexandria, and developing centres, like Piraeus and Ermoupolis, in Syros. In the early 20th century, the migration wave was directed towards the US and Canada.After the war, the population of Andros rapidly abandoned the island, headed to the capital for higher studies and jobs in new sectors. The history of Andros can be traced back in the neolithic period

Travel and Tourism

The beautiful island of Andros is one of the closest islands in Athens. Tourism in Andros is very popular particularly among the Athenians and visitors looking for a short ferry trip from the Greek capital. Its gorgeous landscape and scenery are the main attractions of Andros, offering an ideal destination for your summer vacations in Greece. Andros tourism is an ideal break from the busy capital. There is no tourist office in Andros, therefore all the tourism information are obtained from the numerous travel agencies in the capital. Apart from the main police station there is no tourist police office that offers exclusive assistance to the foreign visitors. For any help visitors can take advice from the police station in Andros

The combination of blue and white, windmills and scenic geography give to the island its famous Cycladic beauty.

Nevertheless, Andros island goes beyond that. It is an exception among the islands of the Cyclades: combined to the traditional Cycladic elements are successive ranges of mountains with steep slopes which are separated by ravines, deep gorges, riverbeds and three verdant valleys planted with olive trees, figs, oranges, lemons and vineyards. One of these valleys is Dipotamata, a lush green area to the south east. Sandy and pine-shaded beaches complete the lovely picture.

As a unique Cycladic island, Andros combines upland greenery with fine sandy beaches, organised or deserted, beautiful mountain villages and seaside ones as well as numerous water sources, such as the ancient springs of Dionysus and small waterfalls. In fact, Andros is famous for its pure water, which is bottled under the trade of Sariza.

Gavrio is Andros main port where all the ferries from Rafina arrive. Its capital is Hora, or Andros town, which is also the second most important harbour of the island. Because of its proximity to the second most important harbour of Athens, Rafina, the island of Andros has become the favourite week-end destination of the majority of the Athenians. The friendliness of its inhabitants adds one more important element to the list of the numerous charms of Andros.

Travel to Andros island

Travel to Andros island, Greece: The island of Andros is easily accessible by ferry from the port of Rafina, on the north eastern side of Attica. There is no airport in Andros but the closest is the International Airport of Athens that receives many internal and external flights.

Here are travel information about the nearest airport and flights, ferries but also useful numbers, pdf guide and information about our travel services.

Flights near Andros

There is no airport in Andros. The closest airport is on Athens, the capital of Greece. The airport of Athens receives flights from most airports of Greece and from many international airports. From the airport of Athens, you take the bus or taxi to the port of Rafina, located about 30 min from the airport. From Rafina, there are daily ferries to Andros.

Ferries to Andros

There is no ferry to Andros from Piraeus, the main port of Athens. A ferry to Andros departs from the port of Rafina, on the northern side of Athens. Rafina is the closest port to the International Airport of Athens. There are buses and taxis to connect the Athens Airport to the port of Rafina. A ferry to Andros from

Rafina takes 2 hours. There are daily Andros ferries from Rafina all year round, but schedules are more frequent in summer. There are also ferries from Andros to: Mykonos island, Tinos island, Syros island, Lavrio island, Kythnos island and Kea island. For information about these locations, visit our section of Greek islands

Travel services in Andros

Use our travel services in Andros and organize your holiday to this beautiful island of Cyclades. Have a look on the Andros hotels that we suggest or book your ferry tickets through our online system. If you need to rent a car in Andros, also make a car reservation. If you do not wish to get into all these details, just ask us to plan your holiday tri

Andros Architecture

About the architecture of Andros, Greece Andros is a very interesting island of Greece probably because it is not a typical example of Cycladic architecture but rather a mixture of different characteristics. Typical Aegean type houses that coexist with neoclassical buildings, Venetian towers and fortresses, towers like the Hellenistic Tower of Agios Petros, old watermills and fountains create this beautiful setting of unique harmony.

The architecture of Andros has many aspects but it is especially known for the cosmopolitan atmosphere and the cultural identity that preserves the last decades. Around the Chora of Andros and the picturesque villages, one can see perfect examples of rural houses standing close to Venetian towers.

Equally impressive are the beautiful mansions that can be found around the island which were built during the Turkish rule painted with different colors. Another characteristic of Andros island is the many dovecotes that adorn the island and can be found mostly in Korthi region. Stone structures built in geometric shapes forming triangles, diamonds and circles give the island a beautiful tone.

Visitors will find many hotels in Andros that have been created in respect of the traditional Cycladic architecture

Festival

Festivals and cultural events of Andros In the beautiful island of Andros, surrounded by the colourful flowers, religious feasts re highly appreciated by the locals and the tourists. Visitors taste the local food that is distributed at the church yard at noon. Andros organizes a plethora of festivities on the name day of many saints, with lovely ceremonies in the picturesque churches and at the squares where visitors offer food and wine. For the major feasts, a Holy Mass is conducted followed by a procession around the village. After the litany, people are gathered in the square to eat, drink and dance till the early morning hours. The most notable feasts in Andros are:

Religious feasts

August 15th

On the 15th of August, the feast day of Virgin Mary is celebrated with local events in Pano Katakolo, in Panachrantos Monastery in Korthi, in Mesaria and finally in the small chapel of Panagia Thalassini, in Chora. There is a big fair that includes music, dancing and feasting till dawn.

Panagia Theoskepasti

Another religious festival that is worth seeing in Andros is on the name day of Panagia Theskepasti, two weeks before Easter.

Day of Zoodochos Pighi

The feast day of Zoodochos Pighi, on Friday after the Easter Sunday.

July 17th

On 17th of July, locals celebrate the feast day of Agia Marina, in the old and abandoned monastery of Agia Marina. On that day various ceremonies are held and the island organizes a great festivity with local dances.

Cultural Festivals

Gavriotika Festival

Gavrio is home to Gavriotika Festival which marks the beginning of the summer festivals. The event involves art exhibitions, folklore items, sports games and other events.

Carnival

A traditional feast which is worth seeing is the Carnival Parade of Gavrio which takes place on the last Saturday of the Carnival festivities. Local treats are offered to the visitors.

Korthiana Festival

During August, the cultural festival of Korthiana takes place in the village of Korthi.

Ploes Festival

The famous Ploes Festival is organized by Petros and Marika Kydonaeus Foundation and highlights the musical and art events presented in Andros

Churches

Guide to churches in Andros island, Greece Andros is home to numerous Byzantine churches and monasteries. Their beautiful architecture, large size and impressive mosaics witness its great development during the 11th and 12th century. Zoodochos Pigis is the largest monastery in Andros located in Batsi village, west of the island's capital. Well-protected by strong walls, almost like a fortress, the monastery offers an amazing view and is open to the public.

Above the main port rises the whitewashed church of Panagia Theoskepasti, the saint protector of the island. The chapel of Panagia Thalassini is regarded as the symbol of Andros, built on top of a rock. The

Monastery of Papachrantos is one of the oldest monasteries in Andros with beautiful architecture. Equally noticeable are the well-preserved monasteries of Agios Nikolaos and Panagia Tromarchiani.

Panagia Theoskepasti

The church of Panagia Theoskepasti in Andros Cyclades, Greece: The church of Panagia Theoskepasti is located on top of a hill in the quarter of Paraporti in Chora, the capital of Andros, few metres from Kairi Square. Legend has it that in a dark night, the locals saw a dazzling light moving from the sea towards the coast. It was an icon of Virgin Mary that went directly into a cave by itself when it reached the coast. The locals transfered the icon to the church of Agios Athanassios, but the next morning the icon was miraculously found again into the cave. That is when people decided to build a church above this cave and place the icon in there.

The church was built with the contributions of the locals but due to limited sources, the roof was not finished for a long time. This is when a second miracle happened and many tree logs were washed out one night from the sea. These logs were used to construct the roof. As it was believed that God sent the logs, the church was named Theoskepasti, which means roofed by God.

The miraculous icon of Virgin Mary can today be seen in the iconostasis of the church. Except from the faces of Virgin Mary and baby Jesus, the entire icon is later covered with silver. The iconostasis is golden and it is decorated with reliefs, made by an artist from Chios in the 17th century. There are not many frescoes inside the church, but there are rare Byzantine icons on the walls.

The church of Panagia Theoskepasti is a three-aisled basilica and has two tall bell-towers. It is considered the protector of the entire island of Andros and also the protector of sailors. The church celebrates on the fifth Friday after Lent Monday (Friday of the Akathist Hymn).

Other Churches

Panagia Thalassini

Panagia Thalassini

Bell tower Source

Seaside chapel

Lovely church

Countryside

Blue dome

Church in Batsi

White church

Villages

Andros is an island that distinguishes for its traditional architecture and the lovely nature. Chora, the capital village, has pure Cycladic architecture and some

Neoclassical houses. In the inland, small mountainous villages dot the landscape, while the coasts are lined by seaside settlements. Many hotels and accommodation are located around these villages. After you have seen the best Andros villages

Discover our guide to 7 Andros villages. They are all presented with detailed description

Chora Village

The history of Hora begins from the times of the Venetian rule. It was a small settlement under the protection of the castle whose ruins can still be seen at the Cape. In the beginning, the settlement was connected to the castle by a wooden bridge which was later replaced by the existing stone one. The entrance to the castle can be seen today and is still the main entrance to the old city. The picturesque old city of Andros, Hora, maintains its original medieval road layout and the architecture is an excellent example of a combination of Byzantine, Venetian and neoclassical styles.

The town started to slowly expand outside of its ancient walls, flourishing especially at the start of the C20th when the ship owners of Andros controlled almost a quarter of the Greek merchant fleet. It was during this time that the beautifully elegant neo-classical mansions were built making Andros, Hora, one of the most charming capitals in the Aegean. The moderate tourist development is mainly in the area of Emborios..

Here you will find most of the accommodation to rent, restaurants and clubs. There are two beaches in Hora that can be reached by foot. To the south is the beach of Paraporti and to the north is the beach of Nemborios. A further very picturesque beach is 20 minutes walk from the track that begins at the end of the beach of Paraporti, taking you to the beach of Lidi.

Two other beaches worth visiting are the beaches of Gyalia and Piso Gyalia which are about 15 minutes drive from Hora.

In the summer months you should take a boat trip to the beautiful beach of Achla where the river Achla empties into the sea, creating a wonderful wildlife sanctuary that sees many varieties of flora and fauna as well as hundreds of visiting migrating birds

Andros Town has two squares: the first one is stone paved and surrounded with many cafes, little restaurants and pastry shops, all shadowed by a huge plane tree. The second square is paved with marble, has a statue of the Unknown Sailor and an amazing view of the sea and the rest of the town.

Because it is located at the tip of the peninsula, this square is the best place to go to see the beautiful Venetian-style stone bridge connecting Andros Town to a little islet supporting the remains of an old castle, built during the Venetian period in order to protect the city. The colorful houses and wonderful Neoclassical mansions add even more beauty to the town.

Hora is also the cause of the artistic reputation of the island, since it is housing many fine museums from which the Museum of Modern Art exposes, every summer, works of famous Greek and international artists.

Andros Town is located at 35 kilometers east of the harbor (Gavrio). From there, some lovely and picturesque villages can be reached, such as Messaria, a lovely medieval village, Menites, Stenies and Apoikia, where the famous Sariza spring is situated.

Sightseeing

Goulandris Museum of Modern

The Goulandris Museum of Modern Art in Andros Cyclades: The Museum of Contemporary Art of the

Basil and Elise Goulandris Foundation was established in 1979. The museum showcases the works of the renowned sculptor, M. Tombros, originating from Andros. The Museum also has a fine collection of works of renowned Greek artists. The Greek collection in particular is constantly updated with newer inputs, while it has also been showcasing the works of renowned international artists

In July 1986, the museum launched its new wing and over the years this new section has hosted numerous international art exhibitions and has successfully showcased the works of legendary artists of the stature of Picasso, Matisse, Kypka, Kandinsky, Henri Cartier-Bresson, Balthus and Paul Klee.

To attract the attention of the art connoisseurs Greek, pieces of work from artists like Bouzianis and Galanis too have been on display at the museum. The Museum over the years has established a close working relationship with the renowned National Gallery of Athens so as to provide an unmatched art exhibition platform on the island of Andros

Nautical Museum

The Maritime Museum of Andros, Greece: The Maritime (or Nautical) Museum of Andros is housed in an elegant Neoclassical mansion in Chora, in the square of the Unknown Soldier. Its location gives excellent view to the Aegean Sea and may work symbolically to connect the sea, the museum and the long maritime tradition of the locals, who had always been connected to the sea as traders, fishermen or seamen.

The Maritime Museum of Andros was established in 1972 and has a rich collection with nautical items from the ancient until modern times such as shipping documents, models of old and new vessels, nautical dairies, costumes and many other exhibits that depict the strong connection of the locals to the sea

Kydonieos Institute

Kidonieos Institute in Andros Cyclades, Greece: Kydonieos Institute is a non profit foundation established in 1994 in Chora, the capital of Andros. Over the years, Kidonieos has become the cultural and spiritual center of the island hosting art exhibitions, musical concerts, theatrical shows and literature meetings. Its main objective is the promotion of cultural events and exhibitions in Andros. Since 1997, Kidonieos occasionally provides free pottery workshops for children and adults

Since 1995, Petros and Marika Kidonieos Foundation is organizing a special event called Ploes that takes place every summer introducing important painting and sculpture exhibitions. Ploes has become an integral part of the institute as it supports the cultural and musical events of the island. Kidonieos Institute constitutes a special tribute to newer and contemporary versions of post-war Greek art, through selected and representative works of renowned artists

Panagia Theoskepasti

The church of Panagia Theoskepasti in Andros Cyclades, Greece: The church of Panagia Theoskepasti is located on top of a hill in the quarter of Paraporti in Chora, the capital of Andros, few metres from Kairi Square. Legend has it that in a dark night, the locals saw a dazzling light moving from the sea towards the coast. It was an icon of Virgin Mary that went directly into a cave by itself when it reached the coast. The locals transfered the icon to the church of Agios Athanassios, but the next morning the icon was miraculously found again into the cave. That is when people decided to build a church above this cave and place the icon in there.

The church was built with the contributions of the locals but due to limited sources, the roof was not finished for a long time. This is when a second miracle happened and many tree logs were washed out one night from the sea. These logs were used to construct the roof. As it was believed that God sent the logs, the church was named Theoskepasti, which means roofed by God.

The miraculous icon of Virgin Mary can today be seen in the iconostasis of the church. Except from the faces of Virgin Mary and baby Jesus, the entire icon is later covered with silver. The iconostasis is golden and it is decorated with reliefs, made by an artist from Chios in the 17th century. There are not many frescoes inside the church, but there are rare Byzantine icons on the walls.

The church of Panagia Theoskepasti is a three-aisled basilica and has two tall bell-towers. It is considered the protector of the entire island of Andros and also the protector of sailors. The church celebrates on the fifth Friday after Lent Monday (Friday of the Akathist Hymn)

Activities and Entertainment

Aporthito

Aporthito is a charming cafe-bar tucked away in one of the paved streets in Chora. Due to its hidden location, the cafe receives only a few people every day and these are mostly tourists. Aporthito is actually a perfect spot to hang out and drink a cup of coffee or a juice in a quiet atmosphere while you watch people making a stroll around the narrow streets of the island. The cafe serves also delicious pancakes, as well as froutali (an omelet made with local sausages and potatoes), and a selection of traditional desserts, including amigdalota, a kind of almond candy that is popular in the Cyclades

Heaven

Chora Heaven Cafe, located in Chora, is a favorite hangout. Here, you can taste a wide choice of drinks, refreshments and coffee, as well as a fairly good selection of pancakes and crepes. This popular coffee shop is found in Kairi Square, at the end of the long street leading to the beach Source: www.greeka.com

Cabo Del Mar

Located within a close distance from Chora, in the quarter of Nimborio, Cabo Del Mar is a popular bar-restaurant. It is housed in a splendid stone neoclassical building offering a view to the sea. It suggests innovative dishes with traditional recipes and local desserts. The cuisine of Cabo del Mar follows the principles of creative gastronomy, influenced by the Mediterranean flavors. The resident DJ spins some great numbers to keep the foot tapping until the small hours. The outdoor bar is a lovely place with extraordinary sunset views and chill out music, offering a vast collection of wines and cocktails

Parea

Parea is a picturesque restaurant in Chora that captivates every customer. There you will enjoy dishes from the Mediterranean and local cuisine in combination with great views to the sea. Just above the beach of Chora, this restaurant has warm decoration and friendly service. This is the ideal place to spend a night with friends and family, with tasty traditional mezedes, fresh salads and delicious main courses

Ballas George

George is a traditional restaurant located in the capital town of Chora offering a relaxed ambience for a family visit. The minimalist decoration and the delicious cuisine is a mix of traditional Andriot and international cuisine. The signature dishes include the "lambriati", a lamb or veal dish cooked in the traditional oven with entrails, rice, cheese, eggs and mint, or the tasty roasted chicken and veal dish. Their seafood mezes are prepared from fresh catch and are a must try. They offer an excellent choice of local wines and some international too. The prices are affordable and the service is excellent

Batsi Village

Batsi Village Andros: Batsi is also part of the municipality of Hydroussa. It is located 7 kilometers away from Gavrio, separated from it by beautiful sandy beaches, small picturesque harbors and hidden coves. Like Gavrio, Batsi used to be a fishing village.

It has now become the touristiest place of Andros and is therefore the major resort of the island. Despite its touristy character, Batsi has kept a traditional and picturesque charm. This attractive town has little red-tiled colored houses which have been built amphitheatrically, and encircles a bay with a lovely fishing harbor at its south end and a nice sandy beach at the other side.

The town is cosmopolitan but maintaining the local colors, and a main destination for the visitors. It therefore has all the expected and necessary comforts for nice holidays: taverns, ouzo shops, night-time entertainment, tourist agencies, hotels, room for rent, post office, bank, car and motorbike hiring agencies and many shops

Gavrio Village

Gavrio Village Andros: Gavrio is part of the municipality of Hydroussa. It is the only active port connecting Andros to Rafina, and it is located on the west coast of the island. Gavrio was a fishing village until 20 years ago, when it started to slowly develop its tourist infrastructures. Restaurants, taverns, bars, cafeterias, hotels, camping, rooms for rent, tourist offices, car and motorbike hiring offices and many shops welcome the visitor, making it easier for him to enjoy his holidays.

The main settlement of Gavrio can be quite simple and picturesque when the port traffic calms down. Gavrio is the starting point of excursions towards the north of the island on search of fine sandy beaches and picturesque villages. Towards the south of Gavrio some golden beaches can be found as well as the amazing old tower of Agios Petros.

From Gavrio one can reach the Monastery of Zoodochos Pigi, many fine sandy beaches, and some villages such as Fellos, Makrotantalos, Amolochos, which used to be the capital of the area during Turkish occupation, Chartes, Varidi, Kalivari, Ano Agios Petros, Yides, Kalokerini and Vitali.

Sightseeing

Hellenistic Tower of Agios Petros

The Hellenistic Tower of Agios Petros in Andros Greece, Cyclades: The tower of Agios Petros is a quite well-preserved tower, placed on a hill overlooking the bay of Gavrio. It was probably built in the Hellenistic Era, in the 4th or 3rd century BC, and is 20m high. It has a cylindrical shape and was constructed by local schist. It used to have five floors, connected to each other with a helical ladder

As we conclude from the area of its construction and its shape, the tower was built to overlook the above sea routes. People wanted to control the sea surrounding Andros island so that they could protect themselves and their villages from an enemy invasion or an attack by the pirates

In fact, the area had copper mines, which worked from the ancient times till the mid 20th century, and was thus economically-developed. Therefore, the tower was useful to protect the mine workers and this source of richness for the island. The tower can be reached from Gavrio town. A 15 min drive and some walking are required to go to the top of the hill and get a view of this ancient tower

Activities and Entertainment

Gavrio Cafe

Apomero

Apomero is a perfect spot to enjoy a vibrant atmosphere, among the crowd of tourist hub. The small terrace offers spectacular views to the island and the deep blue Aegean Sea and it is a great spot to enjoy a coffee or drink

Apomero is a fantastic cafe is located in Gavrio, the bustling harbor of Andros. It is a perfect spot to enjoy a vibrant atmosphere, among the crowd of tourist hub. The small terrace offers spectacular views to the island and the deep blue Aegean Sea and it is a great spot to enjoy a coffee or drink. The cafe has big screens for the best sporting events and internet facilities as well. Besides coffee and drinks, they offer a small selection of light dishes, including crepes and pancakes, as well as the ubiquitous fourtalia, prepared from locally made sausage, egg and potatoes. It is mostly a reference point for the young crowds who enjoy this lively side of the island

Memory

At our cafeteria you can enjoy your coffee or beverage, while enjoying the view of the Port of Gavrio. We are open all day and all year round. We are expecting you and we promise that we will be a Memory of Andros to you!

Cafodion Source

Just across the port of Gavrio, there is Cafodion a cozy cafe-bar for all tastes, inviting you to spend relaxing moments in a spot where every customer will find his corne

Just across the port of Gavrio, there is Cafodion a cozy cafe-bar for all tastes, inviting you to spend relaxing moments in a spot where every customer will find his corner. Sit on the modern mat sofas, try the delicious sandwiches and travel in the sounds of lounge music or choose one of the 30 cocktails. A Greek coffee would be ideal for the traditional types. As for the night, get inside Cafodion to listen authentic jazz-rock sounds while drinking a beer until the late hours. The cafe is mostly frequented by the tourists who make short trips to Andros. Except the drinks it offers local delicacies from Andriot cuisine and special desserts with the signature of tradition.

Menites Village

Menites Village Andros: The settlement of Menites on Andros Island is situated about 6 kilometers from the capital, Chora. Another settlement by the name Mesaria is also nearby. Menites is a beautiful village built on Petalo Mountain, 200 meters above sea level. The village of Menites is famous for its springs and abundance of water and greenery.

Menites village is a trekker's paradise in the true sense of the term; it has impeccable paved alleys and footpaths ideal for trekking. Other good trekking options are towards the Panachrantou Monastery, Pitrofos-Paleopoli and Lamyra-Chora. These spots are easily accessible on foot and are wonderful for relaxation.

The Feasts for Dionysos is celebrated at Menites village with much fanfare. Amygdalota is an excellent sweet preparation, which is synonymous with this feast. The Springs of Dionysus are a major tourist attraction in Menites village and are truly an architectural inspiration. They are actually fountains adorned with lion head motifs.

Sightseeing

The Cyclades Olive Museum in Andros, Greece: The Cyclades Olive Museum is a private museum located in the mountainous village of Ano Pitrofos, very close to Menites. This museum is housed in a traditional building that was bought and restored by civil engineer Dimitris Chelmis, originating from Pitrofos and personal guide to the museum.

The old oil mill that houses the museum is part of a two-floor building and occupies a large part of the ground floor (called katogi). The upper floor used to host the home of the owner. This fine example of animal-powered olive oil producing mill was very frequently met in the countryside of Andros island, operating until the 1960s.

The building of the Cyclades Olive Museum dates from earlier than 1857 and was probably operating during the 18th century. Its architectural elements, like arches and domes, are common in rural architecture of Andros and generally in the Cyclades islands. Until 1967 the oil mill stopped operating and until 1997 it was used as a storehouse.

That year, the entire building (oil mill and house) was bought by its present owner, Dimitris Chelmis, and it was later restored and transformed into a museum. Visitors can get a view to the traditional oil production method in Andros and learn a lot about local culture. A video with an animal powered olive oil production has been filmed in the museum and is screened to visitors.

Springs of Dionysus

The Springs of Dionysus are located along the way from Chora to Stavropeda area, via a slight detour through Menites village. The area around Dionysus Springs is picturesque with beautiful landscapes of fountains and old trees. It is a lush green area and really great for trekking. This region is associated with the ancient culture and in particular the Dionysian worship. People in the ancient times used to believe that the springs gushed from the ancient Temple of Dionysus and that they flowed with wine during the day of his celebration.

Indeed, recent excavations have unearthed the remains of an ancient temple very close to the springs. The mineral water that gushes out of the lion head statues today is said to have therapeutic properties. In the antiquity, the water that used to flow from the crevices in the rocks was carefully collected. As it was a sacred liquid, it was used strictly for ritual purpose and not for any ordinary use.

Ormos Village

The village of Ormos is the centre of the municipality of Korthiou and it is located in the centre of the region and by the seaside, in the southern part of Andros. This attractive small town is ideal for relaxation but has at the same time lots of entertainments options, being the centre of tourism and business in the area.

Here, one can find shops, restaurants, bars, cafes, post office, doctors, chemists, banks, accommodation and an interesting folklore museum. Three fine sandy beaches surround Ormos: Milos beach, which has a wind-surfing school, Vidgi-Agia Ekaterinis beach and the distinctive beach called Tis Grias to Pidima (The Old Lady's Leap). Some old traditional footpaths lead to picturesque pigeon-houses.

The nearby valley of Dipotamata is also worth the visit, with its unique watermills, an area of a great natural beauty, transformed in an ecological museum of water-power. Near Ormos is situated the fine village of Kaparia with its lovely dovecotes, watermills and old stone houses. The villages Vouni, Gianiseo, Lardia, Piskopio with their old churches, stone bridges, watermills and windmills, cool springs, plane trees and old stone houses. There is also Chones, Alamania, Kochilou where is the beautiful Venetian Upper Castle (Pano Kastro) or Faneromeni Castle and the village of Sineti located in an amazing gorge

Activities and Entertainment

Ormos Cafe

Centro Cafe

Centro Cafe Bar is located in the village of Ormos, an attractive tourist spot offering plenty of entertainment options. Centro Cafe is located on the seafront offering spectacular views to the sea. The cafe is mostly popular among the young crowds as the perfect hang out. It boasts a relaxing environment to enjoy a coffee or a drink. Apart from its popularity as a coffee shop it serves also local delicacies, like fourtalia. When the sun sets, the café is transformed into a vibrant place where the beats of music have the first word. For those who are interested, there is a folklore museum near by

Blue Cafe

Blue Cafe is located in Korthi, a picturesque village of Andros and a popular tourist resort, especially for families. The cafe is situated in a pedestrian area among a large string of restaurants and bars, behind the seafront. Blue Cafe serves a variety of coffees, great snacks and seafood mezedes. It is a cozy place and popular among locals and tourists. Here, you have the chance to eat Fourtalia, one of the most known specialties in Andros

Restaurant

Sea Satin Nino

The Cafe

We offer you the best coffee, either it is the most unusual frappe you've ever seen, a Macchiato with whichever flavor you can think of, a hot white chocolate with pistachio, or a simple Greek coffee.

The Restaurant

We prepare Greek / Mediterranean dishes and dreamy desserts from both traditional and contemporary cuisine. Our chefs present new dishes every day. You'll find appetizing dishes, like our seafood platter for ouzo and our famous T-Bone steaks to enjoy in a relaxing atmosphere.

The Bar
Good cocktails are not just "drinks", they're alchemy and Giannis is our Alchemist. His specialties are Caipirinhas and frozen fruit Margaritas. His bar is stocked with the finest spirits and freshest fruits. Cocktails can be enjoyed in our comfortable bar or under the moonlight in our outdoor dining area. Source: www.greeka.com

Noka in Andros

About Noka Established in the area since 1989, the Nautical Club of Korthi, which started by teaching children how to swim, has grown by leaps and bounds to become the most reputed water sports club in

Andros offering world class coaching in a variety of water sports, including wind surfing.

The training team is led by George Frank and Nick Garlic, highly proficient in the sport, and who have bagged several gold medals at the Pan-Hellenic Games as well as many other national and international tournaments. In addition to sports, the center also takes a keen interest in organizing cultural and social activities to promote the rich history and culture of Andros.

Stenies Village

Stenies Andros: Located about 4 km north west of Chora, Stenies is a small beautiful village with traditional architecture. Stone houses and paved streets are the main characteristics of this village, which is built on the slopes of a hill and it is surrounded by few green trees. Although it is close to the capital village, Stenies is not developed in tourism and keeps its authentic character.

In close distance, there are the two beaches of Gialia and Piso Gialia, with few hotels and taverns by the sea. An interesting sight to see in Stenies is the tower of Bisti-Mouvela, a three-storey building of the 17th century, and the church of Agios Georgios close to the tower, with a lovely fresco that dates from 1737.

Restaurant
About Barbarola Barbarola is a beautiful restaurant situated in the charming village of Stenies, at the north side of Chora. It is a magnificent spot to enjoy Andriot cooking offering a terrific view to the countryside. The menu includes a fine selection of local delicacies and other specialties like fourtalia, an omelet made with the famous Andros sausages and potatoes. All dishes are made with locally grown products that enhance the strong flavors like Armenia and volaki. The owners of

Barbarola want to retain the old tradition and introduce it to others through the local treats and flavors. The restaurant keeps a vast collection of wines to accompany every meal

Mesathouri Village

Mesathouri Village Andros: The village of Mesathouri is renowned for its picturesque vistas. The locals are warm and friendly. Since the village is densely wooded there are numerous interesting walking and trekking trails that offer a whole new world of nature based exploration.

If you are an avid trekker, you would do well to take the assistance of a knowledgeable guide who can make your trip much more memorable and fun filled with bits and pieces of information that you were probably not aware of prior to embarking on your trekking trip. For the more adventurous, there is always the option of visiting the neighborhood villages of Menites as well as charming Strapourgies

Korthi Andros

Archaeological Museum, the Byzantine churches, the medieval fortress city of PaniKastro, as well as several settlements and monasteries prove that the life of the area continued from antiquity until the present day. The PanoKastro was the strongest and largest medieval city of Andros. It was built by the Venetians on a high plateau north of the Gulf of Korthi at a height of 1800'. It gave shelter to around 1,000 inhabitants and was seen as a very secure stronghold due to its lofty location and strength of structure.

There is a legend associated with the castle that, during the Middle Ages, the invading Turks, in an effort to siege the castle, sent an old woman and her pregnant daughter inside to ask for shelter. The inhabitants welcomed them in and during the night she opened the gates to let in the Turkish invaders. However, her conscience got the better of her because, the legend claims, that following the invasion she committed suicide by hurling herself from a rock into the sea. Today, this area is known as 'The Jump of the Old Woman'.

The area of Korthi is an ideal place for exploring by foot or car. The Bay of Korthi is the economical and tourist centre of the region. Here the visitor will find most of the available accommodation, restaurants, bars and even a summer cinema. Also, the usual amenities of post office, medical centre, pharmacy and banks can be found.

The picturesque town of Korthi lies along the shore where most of the restaurants, tavernas and bars are located. The road behind the seafront is a pedestrianised area where you will find all the public services as well as a market. On both sides of the bay, the beaches are perfect for swimming as well as offering ideal conditions for windsurfing. A windsurfing school is also located here where surfboards can be hired. As is the whole of Andros, Korthi is an outstanding place for walking. There exists a network of ancient footpaths across the region and many of the nearby villages, such as Idonia, Mousionas, Piso Maria and Amonakliou, can be reached by these tracks. Korthi is also connected by bus to Hora, Batsi and Gavrio.

Springs and fountains of Andros

It was not chance that brought the first tourists to Andros during the 19th century: they came here because of the reputation of the mineral water and its curative powers. Since 1841 Fiedler reports seven springs on Andros which had proven restorative powers. In 1902 an Andros historian D. Paschalis, raised this number to ten and he was the first, together with Professor Christomanos, to carry out chemical analysis on some of these springs from 1884.

The most famous spring on the island, Sariza, is found at Apikia, in the centre of village. The beautiful fountain is of unknown date. However, the beneficial qualities of the spring water have been known since long, long ago. The water is diuretic and is believed to cure kidney ailments and stomach problems. Analysis of the water shows that it contains carbon salts of sodium, calcium and magnesium and chloride salts of potassium, sodium, magnesium, aluminium and silicon oxide. The spring water is bottled and is sold all over Andros, as well as the rest of Greece.

The spring Zannakis is found at Menites. The water here is mildly alkaline and it also contains iron. It is an excellent, light table water. During the 19th century the spring water of Zannaki and Agia Irini were exported to Athens, Smirni and Constantinople, using clay containers. Two kilometres north of Apikia there is the church of Agia Irini . Within its grounds exists another, lesser known spring, with water to rival that of Sariza, and it has a similar composition.

The Pertenia is found at Mesa Vouni. The water here is exceptionally light and has a lovely flavour. It takes its name from the belief that the water can disperse kidney stones. A private analysis made on this water showed that the conductivity of the water is hardly 6, perhaps the lowest in all of Europe.

Andros really is covered with springs and fountains. It is impossible to determine the exact number, but there are dozens of them. Some have stone surrounds, others more humble in design and they continuously supply villages and settlements with water to irrigate the farms, even meeting housewives' laundry demands and until fifty years ago the water turned the watermills of the island. Some of them are mentioned on the pages relating to the towns and villages as well as the page about the footpaths.

The Ravine of Pithara

The ravine at Pitharas is found about ten minutes' walk from Apikia. The footpath which leads there is flat and covered in ivy, preparing one for what is to follow. The plentiful water rushes rapidly into the verdant green landscape, creating waterfalls and lakes which abound with aquatic life. Rare species of plants and wild flowers are found growing along the whole riverbed. A little further down, the largest working water mill in the Balkans was to be found from 1863 up until1936.

Remata

Remata is a small and picturesque village found between Katakoilos and Arni. The village is crossed by the Arnipotamos River which descends from the Petalo mountain and flows into the bay at Lefka. The Arnipotamos, which starts its journey in torrents, deep in a densely wooded channel, becomes more gentle as it reaches the village. For its entire course it creates waterfalls and ponds suitable for swimming and supplies abundant streams which irrigate the farmland of the area. It has plenty of aquatic life with eels, crabs and in some places, fresh water mussels. At its highest points, near to Arni, some rare species of butterflies are found in the spring. In former times the Arnipotamos supplied numerous watermills, one of which is the Lebesi family watermill, which is very well maintained up to this day. From this watermill a footpath starts which follows the river, crossing the village and reaching, at its estuary, the graphic and deserted bay of Lefka.

Museum

The Museum of Modern Art : This world famous museum was founded in 1979. It now has a new wing that was opened in 1986 and can accommodate international exhibitions. Among the exhibits that have been hosted in the Museum of Modern Art in Andros are the works of Henri Matisse, Pablo Picasso, Chagall, Balthaus, Toulouse Lautrec and many other famous artists of the C20th.

The Archaeological Museum was built in 1981. It hosts findings and relics excavated from early settlements all over Andros. One of the most well known exhibits is a Roman copy of the famous statue of Hermes made by Praxiteles. Another interesting exhibit is the collection of artefacts from the area of Zagora.

The Kydonieos Foundation was founded in 1994 and it focuses on music, theatre, literature and paintings. Every summer various exhibitions are organised of modern artists.

Near to the Square of Riva, in the old city, is the Maritime Museum of Andros which displays the naval history of Andros via sailors' logs, old photographs, maritime instruments and models of the ships of

Andros. In the square of Korai is located the statue of the unknown sailor.

The Kairios Library holds a wonderful exhibit of around 3,000 volumes from the collection of Theophilos Kairios (1784-1852). Plus a plethora of rare editions, manuscripts, historical archives, objects d'art and a small collection of archaeological artefacts. Every summer musical and literature events are organised in the new exhibition space of the library.

Hiking in Andros

Hiking from Apikia to Stenes and Yialia. Duration about 2 hours.

Apikia is located east of the island and only 7kn from Hora. It is approximately 350 metres above sea level and only 2 kilometres from the sea. This small, well-heeled village has the source of the famous natural spring, Sariza and also very close to a less well known spring which is 2kms away in the grounds of Agia Irini church.

Within20 minutes' walking distance is also the beautiful Ravine of Pithara and close by is the village of Remata which has scenic waterfalls and the large watermill. From the village of Aprikia there is a well maintained paved path which takes you through a beautiful valley which, due to the presence of much water is green and lush. Make sure you visit the charming sea captains' village of Stenies and admire all the beautiful houses.

This village also is the site of the old communal laundry of Pentavrisi which some of the locals still use on a regular basis. Cross the little stone bridge of Leontos to visit the 17th century fortified tower house of Mouvelas. In the same area you are also able to visit the 19th century pasta factory that produced vast quantities of pasta right up until the 1930s and was powered by the largest vertical watermill in the Balkans. The walk ends at one of the beautiful beaches at Yialia where you can recover in the crystal clear waters and snooze on the golden sandy beach.

Hiking from Dipotamata to Pano Kastro and Korthi. This walk that can be done in 4 hours about begins in the village of Syneti and partly follows the old road which was the main connecting road from Hora to Korthi until 1950. Locals call this pathway the 'stone steps' and you will soon realise why as after around 800 metres after leaving Syneti the road separates with the main asphalt road to Korthi continuing whilst to the left a paved and well maintained path descends down to the Dipotamata gorge, an area of great natural beauty.

Take this path which quite soon will lead you to a small river that flows through the gorge with a stone bridge crossing it. Cross over this bridge into the heart of the Dipotamata gogrge and on the other side the stone steps begin to ascend up the valley again. This narrow gorge valley begins in Exo Vouni and ends at the bay of Syneti and within it are sited 37 watermills which, up until the 1930s, were used by locals to grind their staple diet of barley.

As you ascend and come out of the gorge you will pass Pano Kastro on your left, a beautiful Venetian Castle that is well worth visiting. to get there you need to follow the dirt road and take the steps which lead up to the castle itself. After visiting the castle, retrace your steps back down to the pathway that led you up out of the gorge and continue up it until you find yourself in the pretty village of Kochilou. The pathway goes through the village and you should ensure you follow the signs for the footpath until you come out of the village. On exiting the village the pathway descends gently to reach Omos Korthiou,. a seaside village which is in the centre of the municipalaity of Korthi

Archaeological sites of Andros

The ancient Zagora is one of the most important archaeological sites of Andros. An ancient settlement existed here from C10th-8th BC. The settlement was protected by a strong wall of approximately 330' long and10' high. The wall had a gate at the entrance to the settlement. Inside there is a temple that was built in C8th BC and was used until the Classical Years, although the settlement had been abandoned 300 years before. The houses were built of stone and had roofs made of earth. Remains of this settlement can be seen in the Archaeological Museum at Hora as well as a model replica of the settlement.

The Tower of St. Peter is located on the slopes of the mountain under the village of St. Petros. It was built during the C3rd-4th BC but the traces of its foundation are pre-historical. The Tower has at least five levels which can be reached by a spiral staircase. The Tower is topped by a dome which today, unfortunately, is partially destroyed. It is not known exactly what function this tower served but the strongest possibility is that it was used as a beacon to send messages across the island by use of fire. During its history, it is certain that it functioned as a garrison to protect the nearby iron ore mines that existed during these times.

The settlement of ancient Ypsili was developed at the same time as Zagora. The habitation of Ipsili continued on its Acropolis right up until Roman Times. The Acropolis was fortified and there was also a Temple dedicated to Demetra and Persephone. Remains of these can be seen today, although excavations are ongoing and it is planned that this will become an area of great interest for visitors in the future.

Touring

It has regular connections from/to Rafina (1-2 daily during winter and up to 6 in the summer), as well as from/to Tinos - Mykonos. Ports in Chora and Corthi mainly host fishing boats, but also private vessels, while Batsi port operates as marina.

From the area of Gavrio one can access the north and northeast part of the island, where there are agricultural villages with developed stock farming (Fellos, Makrotantalo, Gides, Ammolochos, Varidi, Vitali) and also some of the most beautiful beaches of the island.

Heading towards the south part of the island, you can enjoy a route of exceptional beauty, passing by the busiest and best organized beaches (Agios Petros, Chrisi Ammos), as well as unique archaeological sites. You will first reach the cosmopolitan Batsi, the most touristic fishing village of Andros, where you can find hotels and rooms to let that suit every taste (and… budget), as well as restaurants, coffee houses and bars.

There are also excellent beaches. One of the most enchanting areas in Batsi is Sidari.

Having to your right the islands of Kea, Gyaros, Kithnos and Syros, you continue your way towards Aprovato, where you can visit the organized archaeological site of Ypsili. If you stop at Ano Aprovato, you will get the chance to enjoy a unique view to the Aegean. Here, there is the tavern "Mpalkoni tou Aigaiou" with local cuisine.

Few kilometers to the south you come across Palaeopolis, the ancient capital of the island. In this area there are the only waterfall in Cyclades, the archaeological museum and the site of excavations that still continue. Here you can enjoy a coffee or Greek ouzo.

At Stavropeda, the island's main road is divided in three directions: the left road leads to Chora, the middle one to the picturesque fishing village of Korthi, while the right road leads to Chalkolimionas and Apothikes beaches. From here, the trail to the archaeological settlement of Strofila with the famous rock paintings begins, while in 500 meters, on the road to Korthi and at Agia Triada, there's the road towards ancient Zagora.

Following the road to Chora, you first encounter Pitrofos village, which is built on the slope of Mount Petalo. The vegetation is rich and the mountain's springs provide plenty of water in the area. Before entering Pitrofos, you will come across the 12th century Byzantine church of Taxiarches, while in the village you can visit the Olive Museum, a restored old olive mill. There is also a tavern and a "hip" atmospheric bar.

As you continue towards Chora and before Messaria village, you will come across the road that leads to an exceptionally beautiful green village, Menites. The village's name is originated from "maenads", the nymphs of god Dionysus. In the village's square there are many water fountains that, along with the long-lived trees and the river that flows through the village, create magical scenery. The gurgling of running water, the singing of birds and the rustling of leaves compose a unique symphony. Taverns and coffee houses can also be found here.

Entering the road to Menites but before reaching the village, there is a junction that leads to Strapourgies and Ypsilou villages. Both are leafy and built on the slope of Mount Petalo, having a stunning view of Chora. There are also taverns here. The road leading to these villages ends to the main road of Chora – Apikies, while shortly before the end of it, there is a left detour that leads to Agia Marina monastery.

As you return to the main road to Chora and after passing the Menites crossroads, you reach Messaria, the old "Mesa Meria". The 12th century Byzantine church of Taxiarches is located here, along with several tower houses and the old "Parthenagogeion" (all-female school), which is now converted into a cultural multi-purpose venue. From Messaria you can reach Chora on foot, following unique routes of cobblestone and gravel paths, alongside rivers.

Entering Messaria, there is a detour on the right of the main road that leads to Aladino, Falika, Koureli, Sasa, Zaganiari (all built on the slope of Mount Gerakones) and also to the island's arterial leading from Stavropeda to Korthi. In Aladino village there is a significant architectural monument, the old single-arched stone bridge, which used to connect the road leading from Messaria to Falika. Cave "Foros" is located shortly after the bridge. From Falika you can take the spiral uphill road that leads to Panachrantou Monastery.

After Messaria, on the left and lower slope of Mount Petalo, is Lamyra settlement, which is -literally- covered in green. Here you will find fragrant gardens with beautiful bougainvilleas and shipowners manors of exquisite architecture. The village took its name during the 17th century when the French botanist and traveler Tournefort named it "Myra" ("Myrrh") of Andros.

As you complete the route on the main road of the island towards Chora, you arrive at the capital of Andros. It is built on a peninsula ending in a small island where the medieval castle is situated. In front and onto the left of the castle there is Tourlitis, the only lighthouse worldwide which is built on a rock in the sea. It was built in 1887, destroyed by the Germans during World War II and rebuilt in 1994 by Goulandris family.

The capital of Andros has an impressive architecture with several museums (Archaeological, Modern Art, Nautical, Folklore) and institutions (Kydonieos, Kairios Library). You can enjoy a beautiful walk in the alleys and the paved market, wander next to rivers or entertain yourself in the numerous bars, coffee places and taverns. You can swim in Neiborio and Paraporti beaches, but also do water sports in the Nautical Club. There are churches with wonderful iconostases, such as Panagia Theoskepasti (patron saint of the island) and "Agia Thalassini", a chapel built on a rock.

From Neiborio, the road next to the Nautical Club leads to Stenies and Apikia villages. After approximately one kilometer of uphill route, there is a detour on the right leading to Empros and Piso Gialia beaches, as well as to the green village of Stenies with the river and the dense vegetation. Stenies flourished in the last century due to the involvement of residents in senior and well-paid positions of merchant shipping.

As you return to the main road and head to the right, after approximately 3 km., you arrive at Apikiawith the famous spring of Sariza, the water of which is considered therapeutic. There you can find "Sariza" bottled-water factory, as well as the nearby famous Pythara with its lush vegetation and crystal clear waters.

Heading north towards the top of the mountain, you find the Katakalei settlement with the breathtaking view to Aegean. From there you can take the right road that leads to Agios Nikolaos monastery.

As you continue on the main road you arrive at Vourkoti, the village with the highest altitude on the island. Locals are mainly engaged in agriculture and stock farming. From Vourkoti you can take the road leading to the famous beaches of Achla and Vori.

After Vourkoti, the main road heads northwest towards Batsi. On the way, you come across Arni (with strong farming and agriculture), Remata and Katakilo villages. All of them have lush vegetation and plenty running waters. In Katakilo there are taverns with excellent local food.

You can reach the southern part of Andros either by following the road from Stavropeda to Korthi or heading from Chora to Livadia, Vrachnou, Syneti and from there to Korthi. On the main road from "Stavropeda" you come across Zaganiari (the archaeological site of Zagora is nearby) and Kapparia, which took its name from kapari ("caper") abounding in the area. Before Kapparia, there is the picturesque church of Agios Georgios in "Farali" and a right junction that leads to Plaka beach.

On the way to Korthi and after passing by Ano Korthi, Mousionas, Aidonia (with the traditional water fountain where women used to wash their clothes), you reach Ormos Korthiou, an ideal bay for those who love water sports and surfing. Sailing races are often take place here, like the windsurfing world championship in Mistral class.

The famous beach "Tis grias to pidima" (old lady's leap) is within walking distance. In the area of Korthi there are tower houses of the 17th and 18th century, as well as the historical school of Agia Triada (1813). You can find many hotels and rooms to let, coffee places, restaurants, bars and amazing pastry shops with excellent local products, like those of the regional women association.

Arriving at Korthi, there is a left junction towards Chora. On the way, you encounter Kochylou village, which seems to be "hanging" from the mountain, like a painting. From here you can reach Pano Kastro. Shortly after there is a crossroad leading to Panachrantou Monastery and then Syneti village with its famous "Dipotamata", the 7 km canyon, ideal for those who love hiking. The area has unique beaches, like the secluded Lidi on the north and Syneti with its impressive stalactites next to the sea and the undersea gushing waters.

After Syneti and as you continue the journey towards Chora, you come across Vrachnou (built on the mountain slope, offers panoramic view to both Chora and the settlements situated on the opposite slope of Mount Petalo) and Livadia, a green village located in the verdant plain crossed by Megalos Potamos ("Grand River"), which empties into Paraporti.

Other Sightseeing

Aladino Cave

The cave at Aladino village -4.5 to 5 million years old- is one of the top attractions of Andros and has an area of approximately 500 m2. It consists of five halls, four of which are open to the public. It was discovered in 1932 by Ioannis Petrohilos and mapped later on in greater detail. The cave is an impressive spectacle composed of stalactites, stalagmites, helictites, hanging rocks and colorful limestone.

Location: Just before Chora, at Aladino village.

How to get there: By car. Follow the main road from Stavropeda to Chora. Turn right onto the bypass of Messaria and then right again to Aladino and Falika villages. There are relevant road signs.

The Castle of Chora

It is one of the most important monuments in the capital of Andros. This famous castle was the fortified residence of the Venetian ruler Marino Dandolo, when he conquered the island. It was built in 1207. The towers and barracks of the castle, as well as the Venetian rulers' coats of arms, were well preserved until 1943, when the ferocious bombing by the Germans destroyed it completely. Nowadays, one can only see its ruins.

Location: At the waterfront of Chora, in the Unknown

Sailor square.

How to get there: On foot, from Kairi square.

Pythara

The ravine of Pythara is located in Apikia village. According to the tradition, is also called "Neraidotopos" ("Fairy Land"). The plentiful crystal clear waters create an amazing habitat, forming small waterfalls and ponds which abound with aquatic life. The landscape is lush with rare species of plants and birds, wildflowers and several amphibians. The waters that spring from Mount Petalo in Evrousies irrigate the crops, while from 1863 until 1936 powered "Fabrica", the Balkans largest watermill, at Stenies village.

Location: At Apikia village, just a few kilometers to the west of Chora.

How to get there: Leave the car on the main road and follow the path to Pythara. After 10-minutes' walk, you will reach your destination.

Sariza

The spring of mineral water "Sariza" is found at Apikia village and attracts many visitors due to its curative properties (it helps those suffering from kidney ailments). A few meters to the west, is located the factory where "Sariza" water and soda are bottled.

Location: At Apikia village, just a few kilometers to the west of Chora.

How to get there: At the end of Niborio quarter, in Chora, follow the road on your left to Stenies and Apikia. Those wishing to bypass Chora, they can follow the road to Strapourgies - Ypsilou, from the intersection of Menites village.

Agios Petros (St. Peter's) Tower

The Tower of St. Peter is of great interest for the visitors. It is cylindrical, preserved to a height of about 20 m. and was built during the Hellenistic period (4th-3rd century BC). Its base diameter is 9.40 m. and is constructed entirely from local schist. Inside there is a spiral staircase leading to at least five floors. The tower is built in a very privileged position, as it is located on the plain of Gavrio, offering control of land and sea. Around the monument there are also metal mines (copper), which functioned until the beginning of the century.

Location: At St. Peter village, in the area of Gavrio.

How to get there: By car, following the road from Gavrio to St. Peter village.

Pano Kastro (Upper Castle)

The Upper Castle, also known as "Faneromenis Castle", was built from 1207 until 1233, by the Venetian ruler Marino Dandolo. It is located on a stunning mountain plain north of Ormos Korthiou at an altitude of 585 meters. Nowadays, some parts of the walls, as well as Faneromenis church, are preserved. The scenery is magnificent and the view to the eastern Aegean is unique.

Location: Above Kochylos village.

How to get there: Follow the main road from Korthi to Chora (or vice versa) and reach Kochylos village. From there, take the road to the bottom of the hill where the castle is located and then climb 143 stairs to the entrance.

Zagora

Zagora is one of the best preserved cities of the Geometric period in Greece. Its ancient settlement is located on a remote mountain plain (160 meters altitude) on Zagora peninsula. The excavations that took place from 1960 until nowadays have revealed important finds. Its life began on the 10th century BC and lasted until the end of the 8th century BC. The settlement was protected by a strong wall approximately 100 m. long, 2-4.80 m. wide and 3 meters high. Inside there is a temple that was built in the 8th century BC and was used until the Classical Period, although the settlement had been abandoned 300 years ago. The houses were built of stone and had roofs made of earth (doma). Remains of this settlement can be seen in the Archaeological Museum at Chora, as well as a model replica of a house and a temple.

Location: In Zagora mountain plain, on the west side of the island.

How to get there: On foot, following the relevant path from "Agia Triada" (shortly after Stavropeda) to Korthi. It's approximately a 40-minutes walk. There are path signs and the route is very interesting.

Ypsili

The ancient city of Ypsili was discovered in the early 1980's. Excavations have brought ancient relics to light, as well as the temple in the center of acropolis, buildings, part of the wall and a numerous antiquities. These findings are valuable for the study of Geometric and Archaic period in the Cyclades and generally in the Aegean Sea. The temple in the center of acropolis, probably dedicated to the goddess Demetra, was founded in the 8th century BC and remained active at least until the second quarter of the 5th century BC. Ypsili is the only organized archaeological site in Andros.

Location: At Aprovato village, shortly after Batsi, as we head towards Chora.

How to get there: Very easily, by car or bus. The entrance to the archaeological site is located near the main road of the island.

Palaeopolis

Palaeopolis is the ancient capital of Andros, which flourished from the Classical to the Roman era. Today is a beautiful green village, located on the slopes of Mount Petalo, on which there are probably the only waterfalls of Cyclades. The ancient city was much lower, by the port, whose half sunk pier is seen from the village. Excavations initiated in 1987 and still continue. They discovered three sections of paved roads and two arcades, as well as a Hellenistic period building with monumental propylon and colonnaded courtyard inside. There are also proofs of the existence of post-classical and early Hellenistic phases of this building. The agora seems to have been deserted in the first half of the 7th century. The findings are displayed in the Archaeological museum of Palaeopolis.

Location: About halfway through the main road of the island, leading from Gavrio to Chora.

How to get there: By car or bus. Follow the main road, on which the Archaeological museum is located.

Strofilas

This Neolithic settlement had been discovered in the area of Stavropeda, on the west coast of the island. It is the largest settlement of the Final Neolithic period found in the Aegean and extends over an area of about 25000-30000 m2. The settlement was brought to light by the excavations of the 11th Ephorate of Prehistoric and Classical Antiquities. They revealed a wall of 100 m. length, up to 2 m. height and 1.60-2.00 m. width, as well as impressive clay pots, jars, pots, stone tools, arrowheads, jewelry, figurines, bronze objects, etc.

The settlement dates back to around 4000 BC and is characterized as the largest and best preserved Neolithic settlement of the Aegean. It was densely built-up with early urban structures, involving proportional social coordination. The carved rock shapes representing animals, fish, etc. are impressive, while the ship representations prove that Cycladites were wandering the seas since then.

Location: At the area of Stavropeda, in the center of the west side of the island, in Strofilas mountain plain.

How to get there: The site is not organised and you can get there only on foot. Follow the road right of Stavropeda and then left, towards the path that leads to the mountain plain.

Cultural Art Information

Andros is, without a doubt, an island of culture and art.

Many Andriots excelled in literature and arts, with greater example that of poet Andreas Embirikos. Another exceptional personality was Theophilos Kairis, one of the greatest Greek intellectuals of the 19th century, or Michael Dertouzos, professor at M.I.T. USA, who is considered as the "father" of Information Technology (IT).

Andros still pertains its rich cultural tradition, offering to the public the opportunity to visit several museums and foundations. Every summer, it hosts numerous events that attract thousands of visitors.

Archaeological Museum Of Andros

The Archaeological Museum of Andros was designed by architect Stamos Papadakis and built in 1981, following a donation from the Basil and Elise Goulandris Foundation. It has a projection room, while from time to time there are exhibitions of modern art at the atrium, in co-operation with the Museum of Modern Art of Basil and Elise Goulandris Foundation. The Archaeological Museum exhibits:

-Collection of findings from the Geometric settlement of Zagora.

-Collection of sculptures dating from the Archaic to the Roman times.

-Collection of pre-Byzantine and Byzantine sculptures.

Location: In Chora, at "Theophilos Kairis" square.

Opening hours:

Tel: (+30) 22820.23664 - Fax: (+30) 22820.23664

Archaeological Museum Of Palaeopolis

The Archaeological Museum of Palaeopolis inaugurated in 2003 and is dedicated to the antiquities of Palaeopolis, which was -for twelve centuries- the capital of the island. It is housed in a building, donated to the Community of Palaiopolis by the Basil and Elise Goulandris Foundation. The museum contains collections of sculptures, statues, coins and inscriptions found in the excavations of ancient Palaeopolis.

Location: On the main road from Gavrio to Chora, in the center of Palaeopolis village - 20 km from Chora and 12 km from Gavrio.

Opening hours:

Tel: (+30) 22820 41985

Museum Of Contemporary Art

It was inaugurated in 1979. The initial reason was to exhibit the collection of works by Andros native sculptor, Michael Tombros. The exhibits were further enriched by part of the personal collection of the two founders, Basil and Elise Goulandris, consisting of more than 300 works of distinguished Greek and foreign artists. This first part of the museum is now the Old Wing and hosts sculptures of Tombros, Zoggolopoulos, Chryssa, Nikolaidis, Takis, etc.

From 1983 to 1985, it hosted temporary exhibitions of Greek painters. The increasing attendance and interest on behalf of the public led to the expansion of the museum. Hence, the New Wing, designed by architect Christos Kontovounisios, was inaugurated on July 1986 and situated opposite the Old Wing.

The architectural integration of the building with its surroundings received a distinction in an international competition. The New Wing of the Museum houses a library, a museum shop, a projection room and spaces for international exhibitions. The works of significant modern artists, which are exhibited since 1986 until nowadays, are a benchmark in the cultural scene, introducing both the museum and Andros in the Greek cultural map.

The museum has hosted, among others, artists such as Paniaras, Picasso, Matisse, Karagatsis, Kandinsky, Bouzianis, Balthus, Galanis, Giacometti, Klee, Chagall, De Chirico, Rodin, Joan Miró, Georges Braque, Nikos Hadjikyriakos-Ghikas, Sophia Vari etc.

Location: In Chora, at "Theophilos Kairis" square.

Opening hours

Winter season: November 1st - March 31st: Saturday, Sunday and Monday 10.00-14.00. April 1st - October 31st: Daily (except Tuesday) 10.00-14.00.

Summer season: July 1st - September 30th: Wednesday - Sunday 11.00 -15.00 & 18.00 - 21.00. Monday: 11.00 - 15.00. Tuesday: Closed.

Tel: (+30) 22820 22444 - Fax: (+30) 22820 22490

Web site: www.moca-andros.gr

Maritime Museum Of Andros

The museum was founded in 1972 and the most important of its exhibits are the old freight contracts, insurance contracts, various nautical diaries, where the life of the Andriots on the seas before the 1821 War of Independence is described, lithographs of Andriot ships and the later first stream freighters of Greece etc. The Maritime Museum, along with the square of the "Unknown Sailor", were donated by Nikos I. Goulandris family.

Location: At Chora, just before the "Unknown Sailor" square. Opening Hours Summer season: Daily 8:00 - 22:00

Tel: (+30) 22820 22275 Fax: (+30) 22820 24166

Kydonieos Foundation

Kydonieos Foundation was founded in 1994 by Petros and Marika Kydonieos. Its main objective is the promotion of cultural events and exhibitions in Andros. The Foundation's philosophy aims in two directions, the first of which is to culturally educate people of Andros.

For this reason, the pottery workshop opens in 1997, while since 1994 the Foundation provides Byzantine music lessons to children and adults and since 1998 instrument lessons (mandolin, guitar, piano) to children aged 7-18. In addition, since 1997, it offers scholarships to the Andros' high school graduates who succeed in the entrance examinations of the Greek Universities.

The second direction concerns the events taking place during summer. Since 1995, the Foundation is organizing a special event called "Ploes" that takes place every summer introducing important painting and sculpture exhibitions of famous artists, such as Tsoklis, Pavlos, Takis, etc.

Location: At the entrance of Chora.

Opening hours

Winter season: Saturday, Sunday, Monday, 10.00 - 14.00

Summer season: Daily (except Tuesday), 10.00 - 14.00

During exhibitions: Monday - Saturday 10.00-13.30 & 18.30 - 21.30 Sunday 10.00 -14.00, Tuesday closed.

Tel: (+30) 22820 24598

Kairios Library

Kairios Library was founded in 1987 as a non-profit

private legal entity, thanks to the efforts and persistence of the Andriot historian, Dimitrios I. Polemis. The Library holds around 60,000 volumes of rare publications, manuscripts, and extensive archives referenced to Andros shipping and courts. It also maintains numerous art works, a collection of ancient pots and statuettes, objects of historical value and items of popular culture. There is a book lending service and a children's book department. Kairios Library has established a fully equipped and advanced book binding workshop, offering training seminars and maintenance of old books, documents and folklore objects.

Location: At the entrance of Chora.

Opening hours:

Tel: (+30) 22820 22262

Olive Museum

One of the best preserved old olive mills in Cyclades is the animal-powered olive mill of Dimitris Chelmis at

Ano Pitrofos. The building dates back earlier than 1823 and was restored according to the traditional architecture. This olive mill retains its original equipment and in 1997 was transformed into a museum, where visitors can get a view to the traditional oil production method in Cyclades.

A video with an animal powered olive oil production has been filmed in the museum and is screened to the visitors. It is considered a great example of agricultural heritage, pre-industrial technology and architectural tradition.

Location: At Ano Pitrofos village, 7 km before Chora.

How to get there: On the 5th km of the main road from Stavropeda to Chora, you reach Pitrofos village. Follow the left road to Ano Pitrofos that will lead you to the entrance of the museum.

Tel: (+30) 6932731776

For the visiting hours please see the web site of the museum: www.musioelias.gr

Folklore And Christian Art Museum

It is an old ice factory, which belongs to Mantzavelakis family and was restored and transformed into a folklore museum. The lower level exhibits are from a typical "Andros Home", while the upper level -used to function as an olive mill- is dedicated to the 18th century Christian art of Andros.

During that period, great Andriot painters, whose works are still preserved in various churches of the island, excelled (Theodosios, Nicholaos Mintrinos, D. Bernardis etc.). The area is divided into three sections and aside hagiography, there are references in ecclesiastical silverwork and wood-carved iconostases. Location: Shortly before entering Chora, just behind hotel "Paradise".

Opening hours Summer season: In July, weekends only (10.00-14.00) and in August, daily (10.00-14.00). **Tel:** (+30) 22820 22189

Folklore Museum

The Folklore Museum of Cultural Heritage of Syneti -as its full name is- is housed in the school of Syneti village, built in 1900 with a donation by the national benefactor Andreas Syggros and stopped operating in 1999. Its rooms have been converted into a typical andriotic house with the corresponding furniture, utensils and tools.

Location: At Syneti village, 7 km from Chora.

How to get there: As you leave Chora (heading towards Stavropeda), take the left road to Livadia-Syneti-Korthi. When you reach Syneti, turn left.

Opening hours July - August: Daily 9.00 - 13.00 and 17.30-21.30

Web site: www.syneti.8m.com

Digital Museum Of Andros

The Digital Museum is housed in the residence of Theofilos Kairis. It projects digital content relevant to the island's history, divided into five periods (pre-geometric, geometric, Classic, Hellenistic, Modern). There are video projection equipment and screens projecting documentaries dedicated to the aforementioned historical periods.

Location: At Chora, near "Theofilos Kairis" square.

Opening hours Summer season: Daily 9.00 - 21.00

Tel: (+30) 22823 60200

Beaches Information

Andros has many top quality beaches that suit all tastes. There are fully organized, easily accessible and ideal beaches for families, but also secluded ones. Some with cold crystal waters and others much warmer. There are also plenty sandy beaches, as well as rocky ones for those who love fishing. Further information for the top 28 beaches of the island can be found below.

West Andros

On the western side of Andros, the large sandy leeward beaches are located. They are easily accessible and well organised, while almost all are equipped with sunbeds and beach bars. Traditional taverns can also be found in most of them.

Pisolimionas

Location: In the northwestern side of the island, just a little bit north of Fellos beach.

Special features: It is a large and perfectly quiet beach with pebbles. There aren't any taverns (the closest one is located in Fellos) or canteens. The water is crystal clear, but cold! Ideal for fishermen and anyone who loves being in seclusion.

How to get there: Taking the road to Fellos, you will find the crossroads with the gravel road that leads to Pisolimionas.

Fellos

Location: In the northwestern side of the island, 5 km north of the port of Gavrio.

Special features: Very large beach with crystal clear water, the depth of which varies. It is not organized, but has trees that provide shade and it is considered as one of the best of the island. You can enjoy your meal at the tavern "To Steki tou Andrea" located near the beach.

How to get there: After Gavrio, take the road to Fellos and Ano Fellos that leads to the beach.

Agios Petros (St. Peter)

Location: Next to the main road leading from Batsi to Gavrio, shortly after the "Chrisi Ammos" (Golden Beach).

Special features: It is the island's largest beach, sandy, with shallow waters and quite exposed to the wind. It is fully organized with sunbeds, beach bar and family taverns.

How to get there: Very easily, by car or bus. There is ample space for parking.

Chrisi Ammos (Golden Beach)

Location: Next to the main road leading from Batsi to Gavrio.

Special features: It is the most popular beach of Andros. It is well organized with sunbeds and beach bars with loud music. As its name implies, is covered with fine sand. Its location ensures good protection from the wind.

How to get there: Very easily, by car or bus. There is a rather small parking area. Most of the people park their vehicles on the main road.

Kipri

Location: On the western side of the island, on the main road leading from Batsi to Gavrio, just before "Chrisi Ammos" and right after "Agios Kiprianos".

Special features: Sandy beach, just below hotel

"Perrakis". There are sunbeds, a beach bar and water facilities.

How to get there: By car or bus, taking the main road from the port of Gavrio to Stavropeda, right after "Chrisi Ammos" and before "Agios Kiprianos". There is a parking area.

Agios Kiprianos

Location: On the western side of the island, on the main road leading from Batsi to Gavrio, just before "Chrisi Ammos".

Special features: Small sandy beach, bounded by rocks that offer shade, ideal for fishing. Its landmark is Agios Kiprianos chapel. Diving courses are provided. There is also a tavern.

How to get there: By car or bus, following the main road from the port of Gavrio to Stavropeda. After "Chrisi Ammos" and before Batsi. There is a parking area.

Batsi

Location: At Batsi, one of the most crowded villages of the island.

Special features: Fully organized beach with sand and shallow waters, ideal for families. It provides sunbeds. Many restaurants, cafes and taverns are located here.

How to get there: Very easily, either by car or bus. There is ample space for parking near to the beach.

Batsi–Kolona

Location: At the edge of Batsi village.

Special features: It is small but organized with sunbeds and a canteen. The spectacular rocks on its edge are ideal for sunbathing.

How to get there: Either by car or bus. There is plenty parking space right above the beach.

Stivari

Location: On the western side of the island, after Batsi and towards Chora.

Special features: Small rocky beach, pretty good for fishing. There is also a tavern.

How to get there: By car. Take the road through Batsi and follow the road signs.

Aneroussa

Location: On the western side of the island, after Batsi and towards Chora.

Special features: Small sandy beach, mainly intended for "Aneroussa Hotel" customers but also accessible to anyone. There are sunbeds and a beach bar.

How to get there: By car. Take the road through Batsi and follow the road signs. It is located between Stivari and Agia Marina.

Agia Marina

Location: On the western side of the island, after Batsi and towards Chora.

Special features: Sandy beach with shallow and crystal clear waters. It is not organized but there is a tavern.

How to get there: By car. Take the road through Batsi and follow the road signs. It is located after Aneroussa. Alternatively, you can take the main road to Stavropeda and turn right, before the crossroad to Ano Aprovato.

Palaiopolis

Location: On the western side of the island, at the end of Palaiopolis village.

Special features: Pebble beach. The ancient port of the village, and also first capital of Andros, was located here. The area is full of archaeological finds. The beach is not organized.

How to get there: On foot. Leave the car on the main road and follow the path (check the road signs) towards the beach.

Chalkolimionas

Location: Right in the center of the west side of the island, in the area of Stavropeda.

Special features: Sandy beach with shallow waters. It is surrounded by rocks and is ideal for fishing. There are sunbeds and a beach bar. From ancient to modern times, there were mines running in the area.

How to get there: Very easily by car. Follow the main road towards Chora and, at Stavropeda, turn right and then right again to get to the beach. There is ample parking space.

Apothikes

Location: Right in the center of the west side of the island, in the area of Stavropeda.

Special features: Sandy beach with crystal clear waters, a small and scenic cove, ideal for fishing. There are few sunshades and a beach bar.

How to get there: By car. Follow the main road towards Chora and, at Stavropeda, turn right and then right again to get to Chalkolimionas beach. Approximately half kilometer before the end of the road, there is a gravel road to your left that leads to Apothikes. There is a parking area.

Plaka

Location: On the southwest side of the island, on the road to Korthi.

Special features: Crystal clear and salty waters. There are trees, storage huts for boats (called "konakia") and rocks that make Plaka ideal for fishing. Remarkable traces of prehistoric settlement have been found in the area.

How to get there: By car. Following Stavropeda - Korthi road, approximately 2 km after Zaganiari village, you will reach a right junction towards Plaka (check the road signs). It is approximately 3 km of rather difficult gravel road.

East Andros

On the eastern side of the island you can find possibly the best beaches, though all are exposed to strong northeastern winds. However, on windless days the visitor gets the chance to swim in uniquely beautiful waters.

Korthi

Location: At Korthi village, in the southeastern side of the island.

Special features: It is a large beach with clear blue waters. Strong winds make it ideal for surfing, but hinder those who enjoy swimming in calm waters.

How to get there: Very easily, by car or the local bus service. It is located 14 km from Chora and 35 km from port of Gavrio.

Vintzi

Location: On the southeastern side of the island, in Korthi area.

Special features: Easily accessible small beach with crystal clear waters, ideal for those who love swimming more than sunbathing. It provides cubicles and showers. There is a tavern nearby to enjoy a meal by the sea.

How to get there: Take the road from Ormos Korthiou to the north and after a few minutes you'll get to the beach.

Tis Grias To Pidima ("Old Lady's Leap")

Location: On the southeastern side of the island, on the north part of Ormos Korthiou.

Special features: Its unique characteristic is a tower-like rock formation emerging from the water. It's a rather small beach with both sand and pebbles and crystal clear waters.

How to get there: By car, 10 minutes away from Korthi. However, you won't avoid taking the last 300 meters on foot, following a downhill path. You can also get there by sea, taking a boat from Korthl.

Syneti

Location: On the eastern side of the island, between

Chora and Korthi.

Special features: One of the most beautiful beaches of the island, with pebbles, deep crystal clear waters and sea caves. It is surrounded by mountains that offer shade during the afternoon. It is exposed to northern winds. The "Dipotamata" canyon with its traditional watermills ends here, where also several scenes of the movie "Little England" were filmed.

How to get there: By car, following the main road from Chora to Korthi, turn left to Syneti village and then left again towards the beach.

Paraporti

Location: On the east side of the island. It is one of the two coves that surround the island's capital, Chora.

Special features: A large beach that is exposed to northern winds, which cause strong undercurrents. There is also a tavern nearby.

How to get there: By car, taking the road from Chora or on foot, from Kairi square.

Niborio

Location: At Chora. It is the second cove that surrounds the island's capital.

Special features: Beach with shallow waters, ideal for families with young children. Andros Nautical Club is located here. The port gathers many fishing boats and yachts. It is a fully organised beach with sunbeds, showers, changing rooms, taverns, cafes and bars.

How to get there: On foot, from Chora or by car, following the coastal road to Stenies.

GIALIA (EMPROS And PISO)

Location: On the eastern side of the island, right after Chora, in Stenies village.

Special features: You can choose between pebbles (Empros Gialia) or sand (Piso Gialia). There is a restaurant at Empros Gialia, while Piso Gialia is equipped with sunbeds and a beach bar. You can swim from one beach to the other.

How to get there: Take the road from Chora to Niborio

and then turn left towards Stenies and Apikia. After a few minutes you will reach the crossroad (to your right) that leads to Stenies village. Follow this road until you reach Empros Gialia to your right. You can get to Piso Gialia on foot, leaving the car on the main road.

Achla

Location: On the eastern side of the island, north of Chora.

Special features: It is probably the most beautiful beach of Andros, with fine sand, small white pebbles, magnificent waters, plane trees and a creek that leads to the beach.

How to get there: It is not easily accessible, since there is only a gravel road from Vourkoti village. You can get there much more easily by taking a boat from Chora.

Vori

Location: In the eastern side of the island, near Arni village.

Special features: Sandy beach with crystal clear blue waters and trees that provide shade. Its unique characteristic is the "shipwreck" (a ship stuck in the rocks). It is not organised.

How to get there: Following the road towards Remata and Arni, take the gravel road on your left and turn left again on the first junction.

Ateni

Location: On the eastern side of the island, approximately 7 km away from Batsi.

Special features: It is divided in two beaches. The smaller in size (on the left) is the most popular one, as it is protected by the strong winds, while the larger (on the right) is sandy, with crystal clear waters, ideal for surfing. The latter also provides sunbeds and a canteen.

How to get there: By car. Take the road from Batsi and follow the road signs. The last part of the road is covered in gravel, but it is in excellent condition.

Vitali

Location: On the northeastern side of the island, close to Vitali village.

Special features: One of the best in Andros. It is a large sandy beach that also has pebbles. It has crystal clear waters and rocks providing shade. There are sunbeds and a summer tavern.

How to get there: After Gavrio, take the road to Agios Petros, where you will meet a crossroad that leads to Vitali (left) and Gides (right). Follow the road to Vitali. Almost half of the road is covered in gravel, while the distance from Gavrio is approximately 14 km.

Zorkos

Location: On the northeastern side of the island.

Special features: Large beach, with rich golden sand and crystal clear waters, ideal for those who love fishing. There is also a summer tavern.

How to get there: Half hour route by car from Gavrio.

After Varidi, there are approximately 5 km of good condition gravel road.

.

Peza (Mikri and Megali)

Location: On the northern side of the island.

Special features: Ideal for fishing and for those who love being in seclusion. It is exposed to northern winds, hence it is not recommended during windy days.

How to get there: By car. Follow the road from Gavrio to Fellos, pass the crossroad towards Mermigies and turn left on the next junction. After Sidontas, take the gravel road towards Hartes and from there get to Peza. You can also take the road from Kalivari village.

Sports

Andros has a great tradition in sports. It has been recorded that Aristaechmos Hieronymos and Proklis won the ancient Olympic Games, while in modern times many Andriots played a significant role in Greek sports.

There are several clubs of different sports in the island (mainly football clubs), like Andriakos. There are many football and basketball fields, yet the absence of an indoor hall is evident.

Andros particularly stands out in nautical athletics. The nautical clubs of Andros and Korthi are members of the Hellenic Sailing Federation, having a significant presence in races. Alongside, they have organized major sailing races with great success.

Nautical Club Of Andros

Nautical Club of Andros was founded in 1957 and has active departments of Open Sea Sailing and Sailing Triangles (Optimist and Laser). It is a member of the Hellenic Sailing Federation. Lots of the Club's athletes have gone on to excel in top positions at national competitions, with greater example that of the Andriot Nikos Kaklamanakis, gold medalist in the Olympic Games of Atlanta (1996). The next year, he accomplished the crossing of the Aegean, having as starting point the premises of the Nautical Club of Andros. Every year, on early June, the Club hosts the Andros International Yacht Race with great success.

Occasionally, the Club organises various activities, such as beach volley tournaments, scuba diving lessons, etc. Website: www.noa.com.gr

Contact:

Nautical Club Of Korthi

The Nautical Club of Korthi Andros was founded in 1989 as a non-profit athletic association, based in Korthi. Its main goal is the propagation of nautical sports. It is an active member of the Hellenic Sailing Federation, having departments in windsurfing and swimming. It has a windsurfing team, consisting of children aged 7-19 years old who are trained at Ormos Korthiou. Most of these young athletes have participated and excelled in National championships.

Among others, it hosted the Mistral Junior World Championship at Ormos Korthiou.

Website: www.noka.gr

Contact: Τηλ. 210 4293910 και 22820 24543, email: info@noa.com.gr

Accommodation

Hotels - Rooms Ydroussa

Ydroussa Area

Adonis Guesthouse: Adonis Guesthouse Andros Apartments and Studios is located by the charming beach of Batsi, one of the most beloved destinations in western Andros Greece. All Apartments and Studios of Adonis Guesthouse in Andros feature: air conditioning (a/c), bathroom, fridge, kitchen with the necessary utensils, coffee maker, kettle, toaster, TV, safe deposit box, hair dryer, free Wi-Fi internet access.

Aegea Blue: Ten years of careful research by of the best Greek architects went into the design and development of AEGEA. 24 luxurious and independent villas ranging in size between 40 – 400 m2 were built with the layout and style of a traditional ship owner's village. There are central squares, viewpoints, pathways, a swimming pool, amphitheater, bar , traditional restaurant.

Aegean Castle: The hotel is consisted of only 5 autonomous suites which can accommodate 2 to 4 people. It's ideal for couples, families and large groups and offers a unique vacation experience, by emphasizing on privacy. Aegean Castle offers private veranda with Sea View, LED TV32'', Wi-Fi, Mini bar service, Bioclimatic A/C, hairdryer, iron facilities, private parking.

Aithra: Built on the beautiful beach of Agios Petros on Andros, the housing complex Aethra, it is certain that it can provide a true oasis to anyone who wants to rest. All the houses have big verandas with a splendid view over the sea. We offer air conditioning, tv, wifi, safe box, hair dryer, refrigerator, shower.

Aladou Apartments: Aladou apartments is located in Batsi, one of the most picturesque coastal villages of Andros. It's only a few meters from the sea and nearby there are all kinds of amenities (parking, bakery, pharmacy, restaurants, cafes etc). The apartments surrounded by a large garden with a lot of plants, parasols and benches, a well and a wood stove.

Allegria Family Hotel: The Allegria Family Hotel, built with care and attention, is located 200 m from the largest sandy beach on Andros island. It is found in the seaside settlement of Kato Agios Petros, in a short distance from the port of the island, but still away from busy life. We offer a full equipment kitchen, tv, air conditioning, free wi fi, daily cleaning service.

Althea: The unique architecture, combined with the pristine stonework of Andros, meets the modern face ofluxurious accommodation, in a construct of six autonomous, semi-attached traditional houses - apartments at Andros village Aprovato. All rooms include a fully equipped kitchen, electric Kettle, bathroom, T.V, hairdryer, Wi-Fi.

Almar Apartments: Almar Apartments, at Mpatsi of Andros, are furnished and fully equipped studios, apartments for rent, ideal for holiday-makers seeking relaxing and private family holidays. Each one is a neat and clean apartment, very comfortable with enough space. All of them offer to the customer pure vacation for body and soul.

Alpha Chrysallis: Alpha Chrisallis Studio is located in Paleopolis of Andros, a few meters away from the archaeological Museum, in a place between mountain and sea. All our rooms includes bathroom, air condition, tv, oven, electric cooker, toaster, coffee machine, hood and fridge.

Αμορανι Studios: Just steps from Batsi's village square and 400 metres from the beach, Amorani Studios offers self-catering apartments with beautiful views of the village and free private parking. Relax in your air-conditioned studio and prepare meals in the fully equipped kitchenette. Enjoy breakfast on your private veranda whilst taking in the scenery.

Anastasia Luxury Villas: Select Anastasia Luxury Villas for your holidays and admire the traditional architecture of Andros. It is a set of two buildings, at Ano Gavrio, which blend with the environment of the island. The result is a familiar and cozy atmosphere, tranquil setting, ideal to fully relax and unwind overlooking the endless sea.

Andros Luxury House: This houses is located in the area of Kypri, a place to swim, fish, surf or just sunbathe. All houses have a spacious living room with modern kitchen, a bedroom and an bathroom, a furnished veranda with views of kypri Bay. The houses includes an LED TV, DVD player, a fridge, Electric cooktop/oven, air conditioning, free wi-fi.

Andros Prive Suites: Beautifully nested on the hill above Kypri bay overlooking the fascinating gulf of Gavrio, Andros Prive Suites is an exclusive private escape for our elite guests. The stone and white plaster villas are cascading down the hill, forming four spacious suites with exclusive individual spaces and respect to the privacy of their inhabitants Andros Prive Suites is situated among the most famous Andros island beaches of Saint Peter

Andros Holiday: Andros Holiday hotel is located in Andros, just 400 meters from the port of Gavrio and only two hours away from the port of Rafina. Built in traditional Cycladic architectural style with 78

generously sized rooms all offering a breath taking sea view, and within walking distance of an idyllic sandy beach (15 m), this hotel in Andros is an ideal choice for your holiday destination.

Anemoessa: Anemoessa is located in the cosmopolitan village of Andros, Batsi. Our appartments can accommodate up to five people and there are ideal for a family vacation. They come with a separate bedroom, fully equipped kitchen, private bathroom, television, heating and air conditioning

Aneroussa Hotel: Aneroussa, one of the best hotels in Andros and a symbol in the region, is located between two sandy beaches with crystal clear waters, Delavogia and Ag. Marina, only 800 meters from the picturesque, amphitheatrically built Batsi, the tourist settlement of the island. Aneroussa opened its doors in 1985 and since then it has been offering the best services to its guests.

Archontiko Vardia: At Gavrion, the port of Andros, next to the cosmopolitan beaches, Vardia, Liopesi, Saint Peter, Golden Sands Kipri is located the Mansion of Vardia. In all air conditioned rooms and suites we offer free internet, LCD TV, a kitchen, free parking and free laundry service for guests.

Villa Aegeo: Villa Aegeo has 6 studios, all inclusive with bathroom, A/C, T.V., kitchen facilities. Our clean, comfortable, sunlit rooms with quiet homely atmosphere will offer you a comfortable and pleasant stay in the center of Batsi, a few meters from the central square with the shops, restaurants,clubs , souvenir etc. The sandy beach of Batsi is only 80 meters away.

Villa Arni: Villa Arni is located at Batsi village in Andros Island, just 120m from the sea. Choose one of the nine (9) furnished apartments of our villa and relax enjoying the magnificent view. Apartment / Studio facilities:

bathroom with tub and small kitchen, LED TV, air-condition/fan, central heating and boiler, telephone and free wifi internet access.

Blue Bay Hotel: Blue Bay Hotel is located at a particularly privileged site as it is built at Delavogias beach, one of the most superb beaches of Andros island. Our 8 rooms (25 m2 each) can accommodate 2 people (or 2 adults + 1 adult / 2 children). Blue Bay Village complex is situated at a distance of 800 meters from Batsi and 70 meters from Delavogias beach.

Villa Bonatsa: Villa Bonatsa is located in Stivari, 300 meters away from the center of Batsi and 100 meters away from a beach with sand and pebbles. Batsi is a very beautiful coastal village with sandy beaches, restaurants that offer local specialities, bars and nightclubs. Twin and double bedded rooms are available and include: air conditioning, television, refrigerator, Kitchen, safebox, individual verandas.

Villa Galazio: Villa Galazio is located in the most touristic place of the island, Batsi. The Villa consists of 5 double rooms, 2 three bed rooms and 2 (four bed-suites). Room facilities: Private bathroom, sea view, air conditioning, tv, wifi internet access, safe box, shower, hair dryer, refrigerator, mini bar, coffee machine, kettle.

Villa Giasemi: Villa Giasemi is located in the picturesque coastal village of Batsi, in Andros. Villa Giasemi consists of 4 stylish studios where each can accommodate 2-4 people. All studios have private veranda with wonderful view to the Aegean sea, air conditioning, tv, fridge and kitchenette.

Villa Rena: Villa Rena is located in a quiet area, at Batsi of Andros, surrounded by fir and pine trees. The hotel is 200 meters from the center of the village and 250 meters from the nearest beach. Our complex has 13 apartments. Room facilities: Air conditioning, satellite

TV, refrigerator, Kettle, hair dryer, shower, wi-fi and balcony with sea view.

Blue Dolphin: For unforgettable vacations or short breaks visit Batsi resort in the island of Andros, Cyclades, Greece. Blue Dolphin's rooms combine unique sea view & relaxing environment. All rooms, sited in the 1st floor, are comfortable, have their own bathroom, hot water, telephone, TV, wireless internet, hair dryer, safe boxes, a/c (cold & hot) & mini bar. The seashore and the beach of Batsi is only 150-200 m away.

Blue Era: Offering accommodation with air conditioning, Blue Era Apartments is located at cosmopolitan village Batsi, in Andros. The accommodation comes with a flat-screen TV. There is also a kitchen, fitted with a refrigerator and stovetop. There is a private bathroom with free toiletries in every unit. Towels are provided.

Villa Helen: Villa Helen is located next to one of the most beautiful beaches of Andros. It's a newly built complex that follows the traditional Cycladic architecture and combines a magnificent sea view with all modern commodities. Every apartment offers fully equipped kitchen, washing machine & dishwasher, TV set (living room & bedrooms), Bathroom with bathtub.

Villa Koula: In a 2-hour-journey away from Raphina, VILLA-KOULA is waiting for you, for your escapes. Fully equipped studios with air condition that can accommodate 2-4 persons, located in a green environment, close to the popular batsi beach and about 70m away from the largest super market of the area. A friendly envirnoment is expecting for you for vacations that you" ll never forget.

Villa Limanaki: Villa Limanaki is located in Batsi (Stivari), a picturesque town in Andros Island. It offers a magnificent view of the deep blue sea and promises a comfortable and quiet accommodation. Our premises consist of six two-bed rooms, one three-bed room and one studio (four beds). Room facilities: kitchenette, refrigerator, television, air-condition (cool/heat), parking, cooker.

Villa Maniati: Villa Maniati is a lovely complex of studios and apartments in Andros, located just 150 meters from Golden Beach and St Peters beach. Constructed with traditional Cycladic style, the complex of Villa Maniati has very spacious and convenient apartments and studios in Andros. They are all equipped with air-conditioning, free wifi, TV, fridge, fully-equipped kitchen and balcony or veranda with sea view.

Villa Pitsa & George: Villa Pitsa & George is located at Stivari of Batsi, 300 meters away from the center of the beautiful village and 30 meters from the beach of Stivari. We offer 11 studios/apartments (2-4 people), having each one balcony with unique seaview. We are looking forward to meet you to our friendly family environment for unique holidays.

Villa Sophia: Villa Sofia hotel is located just 250 meters away from the beautiful beach of St. Peter. Twelve spacious cottages framed by six acre garden with a playground and mini football offered for a pleasant stay in the island of Andros. In St. Peter's guests can find traditional restaurants, supermarket, bakery, organized and beaches and watersports

Villa Fiamegou: Villa Fiamegou is conveniently located in Batsi, 300m. away from the nearest beach. It offers free Wi-Fi in public areas, a garden and a terrace overlooking the sea. You will find taverns, cafes and nightclubs just 100 meters away. All rooms are fully air-conditioned and have a furnished balcony with sea view. Each includes a flat-screen TV, sofa and electric kettle.

Elpida: At the Batsi 's magical atmosphere lies hotelelpida, a family run hotel. In about 2.000 m2 of private property, apart from the 14 studios building there is a 600 m2 garden. We offer in every room tv, kitchen, refrigerator, prive balcony with sea view, or garden view. Laundry service is available.

Erato: ERATO APPARTMENTS is located on an amphitheatrical scenery in captivating Batsi of Andros. Only 80 metres away lies the beautiful beach of the village and 150 metres is the centre. One and two room apartments are offered (28 s.q. Studios and 37 – 50s.q. two bedroom apartments). All rooms are fully equipped with cooker, bath, television, big verandas of 12 – 30s.q, Parking and autonomous air conditioning.

Ilios Studios: Ilios Studios are located just 150 meters from the beach in a quiet area, full of trees. They have all the comforts for unforgettable holidays in the beautiful Batsi of Andros. All rooms are equipped with

TV, air conditioning, kitchen, refrigerator. Still have parking.

Ionia Studios: IONIA STUDIOS HOTEL is situated at an exquisite location, on Agios Petros' beach, island of Andros, Cyclades, Greece. Agios Petros ' beach is one of the best places to stay on the island of Andros. IONIA STUDIOS is newly built and designed in the typical local architectural style. Guests will be staying at fifteen (15) fully equipped rooms.

Hotel Karanassos: Hotel Karanassos is located in the cosmopolitan village of Andros, which gathers the main tourist infrastructure of Andros, while retaining the local color and charm. Our rooms are located just 50 meters from the awarded with a "Blue Flag" beach of Batsi. The hotel has 23 fully equipped rooms with bathroom, refrigerator, air conditioning, and a private terrace with beautiful view.

Kipri Apartments: Kipri apartments is located at a area with access to three of the most beautiful beaches of Andros, Kipri beach, Golden Sand beach and Saint Peter's beach. Our apartments may host up to five (5) people families, throughout the whole year and include: bathroom, furnished kitchen, t.v., aircondition, central heating, boiler, telephone and internet access.

Krinos Suites Hotel: Krinos Suites Hotel is a luxury boutique hotel, located in the picturesque coastal village of Batsi, the heart of the Cycladic island of Andros. Krinos Suites Hotel is located inside the historical centre, 20 metres from a beautiful wind-shielded beach and a few minutes' walk from restaurants and bars.

Likio Studios: LIKIO STUDIOS is found at the scenery Batsi, very close to the sea, in a wonderful location just 150 meters from the sandy beach of Mpatsi. The complex is constituted from two buildings which created to maintain the basic elements of the traditional Cyclade's Architecture.

Maistrali Studios: On Mpatsi of Andros we created the Maistrali Studios. Almost on the beach, just 70 meters from the crystal-clear beach with golden sands and watersports, 32 rooms and apartments created to relax you. Full equipment in all apartments with air conditioning, kitchen, fridge, satellite TV, hairdryer, private parking and a recreation room.

Mare Vista Hotel: Beautifully situated with a wonderful view over the bay and port, this hotel is only 200 metres from Batsi's main beach and 600 metres from the centre of the village. Amphitheatrically built in levels, the complex offers a beautiful view of the island from each one of the elegantly decorated and comfortable apartments and their verandas

Hotel Meltemi: Meltemi offers accommodation with free Wi-Fi and a balcony looking out onto the Aegean

Sea. It is 200 metres from Batsi Beach and a 3-minute downhill walk to the village centre. Each of the studios and apartments offer a small dining table and kitchenette with fridge, electric kettle and cooking hobs. They all include air conditioning, a TV and a hairdryer in bathroom.

Niriides Hotel: Amphitheatrically built over the paradise beach of Agios Petros, Niriides Hotel consists of luxury and comfortable apartments (50-70 sq.m), elegantly decorated. All apartments are dual-aspect, with a limitless view to the sea. There is a kitchenette and bathroom in every one of them, tv, free wi-fi and private parking.

Ostria Hotel: Ostria Hotel hotel is on the west side of Andros island, 250m away from the port of Gavrio where the boat reaches. Our rooms have satellite TV, bathroom with shower, balcony or terrace, sea view, telephone, mini fridge, fully equipped kitchen and air conditioning. Parking and free wifi is also available.

Paradise Design Apart.: Located by the sea in the cosmopolitan Batsi, Paradise Design Apartments offers accommodation combining the Cycladic style with contemporary elements. The uniquely decorated rooms are air conditioned and have a balcony with panoramic sea view. Each is equipped with either minibar or fridge, and a private bathroom. Free WiFi, safe box and a smart TV are also included.

Perasma Studios: Perasma Studios is located at Kypri of Andros island, near the port of Gavrion, with access to three of the most beautiful beaches of Andros, Kipri beach, Golden Sand beach and Saint Peter's beach. In our 14 studios we offer refrigerator, tv, kitchenette, bathroom, air conditioning and free internet access.

Perrakis Hotel: Perfectly located in front of two beautiful beaches, with modern renovated facilities and overflowing with warm hospitality the Hotel Perrakis on Kypri bay is one of the most beautiful hotels in Andros, one of the most unique of the Cyclades islands. Comfortable and elegant reception areas, amazing views of the blue Aegean Sea from all 44 of our rooms.

Politis Guesthouse: Politis guesthouse is located at Batsi of Andros, 180 meters away from the village's square and 380 meters from the charming beach. The Apartment and Studios of Politis Guesthouse offers air conditioning (a/c), full equipment kitchen, refrigerator, TV and some of them a splendid view of Batsi.

St George Studios: Near the centre of Batsi lies the St George hotel, especially appealing both to Greek and foreign tourists. St George is build with exquisite architectural design with respect for tradition. Every studio has separate entrance and balcony. The rooms are spacious and bright with high ceilings. The traditional stone floor sits in harmony with the marble kitchenettes.

Studios Irene: By the beautiful and clear beach of Agios Petros (Saint Peter) you will find a family type touristic unit of spacious furnished rooms-apartments, surrounded by a green garden. Each one has air-condition, television, telephone, fully equipped kitchen, private bathroom, parking and independent veranda with a spectacular sea-view.

Hydroussa Studios: The complex "Hydroussa" is located in the heart of the picturesque and cosmopolitan Batsi on Andros island, only 300 meters from the beach. It consists of 6 modern apartments, which can accommodate 2 to 4 people and 3 studios for two or three persons, offering fully equipped kitchen, bathroom, tv, airconditioning, hair dryer, free wifi, daily room service.

Filio Guesthouse: Filio Guesthouse is a beautiful house by the sea of Andros surrounded by a big garden full of mulberries and all day singing leafhoppers. All our fully air conditioned rooms have a small terrace with wonderful sea view and are equipped with a kitchenette, refrigerator and kitchen amenities. Our Lounge beach bar La Cantine is the best relax-place of the island.

Chryssi Akti Hotel: The fully organized three stars hotel Chryssi Akti located in the center of the town of Batsi, in Andros island, in front of the beach only 5 meters away. The friendly personnel shall offer you integrated services and moments of sheer hospitality and relaxation. Hotel Facilities: Swimming pool with bar sun chairs and umbrellas, Jacuzzi, Free wireless internet access, Laundry service.

Hotel Rooms Chora Area

Chora Area

9 Muses: The 9 Muses Hotel is situated next to the cosmopolitan Chora of Andros, offering a unique blend of autonomy, comfort and hospitality in an enchanting part of the island. Choose among the 40m2 mesonettes and studios and enjoy all the facilities of a luxurious hotel. Every morning we offer homemade breakfast, prepared with fresh materials produced in Andros.

Class: Rooms

Tel: +30-22820-24777

Fax: +30-22820-23320

Aegli Hotel: A neoclassical mansion offering traditionally furnished rooms on the pedestrian walkway of Andros' Chora. Hotel Aegli is walking distance from museums, restaurants and coffee shops. The main beaches of Chora are a 5-minute walk away. Free Wi-Fi is available. All rooms are air-conditioned with LCD TV's and satellite channels. Open all year.

Class: Hotels

Tel: +30-22820-22060

Fax: +30-22820-25360

Aiolos Hotel: Aiolos is located in Menites, a village 4km away from Chora, the capital of Andros island. The complex consists of 17 rooms, double, triple and quadruple, that are built on three levels on a hill overlooking Chora, with its beaches and the Aegean sea. Built according to the traditional architecture, the rooms include bathroom, television, refrigerator, air conditioning and wireless internet.

Class: Hotels

Tel: +30-22820-51311

Fax: +30-22820-51472

Andria Suites: The Andria Suites are situated in a traditional Andros house which was built 1838. The complex comprise of three suites decorated to a very high standard, fully equipped, offering a unique luxury feeling. All suites equipped with air conditioning, LCD flat screen tv, fax machine, free internet access, electronic safe deposit box, electric iron & ironing board, fitted kitchenette.

Class: Rooms

Tel: +30-210-8250390

Fax: +30-210-8250145

Andria Studios: Andria Studios are located at Nimporio, the beach of Chora Andros, only few meters from the sea. Our studios can accommodate up 2, 3 or 4 persons. We promise a family type hospitality, close to the main street of Chora, with the museums (archaeological, modern art), taverns, bars etc.

Class: Rooms

Tel: +30-22820-22905

Fax: +30-22820-23409

Androslocation.com: Our new Studios – apartments are located at Chora of Andros.There is a very quiet and calm place! The center of Andros town, (with museums, banks, restaurants, bars etc) is only 300 meters from this location. Each apartment includes a private room with double bed (or twin beds), air conditioning and LCD television, a bathroom and a kitchen with oven, electric cooker, toaster, coffee machine, hood and fridge.

Class: Rooms

Tel: +30-22820-22078

Fax: +30-22820-22078

Anemomiloi Studios

Four comfortable and well-organized studios were built on the serene hill of the Windmill vicinity, next to the main pedestrian street of the beautiful town of Andros or Chora. At "Anemomiloi Studios" we offer you daily cleaning room service, fully equipped kitchen (refrigerator, stove or electrical oven, coffee machine, kettle, juice maker), wifi, air condition, hair dryer, iron and ironing board.

Class: Rooms

Tel: +30-22820-24084

Fax: +30-22820-24084

Afroessa Rooms: The rooms and apartments AFROESSA are found in a green all around environment. We offer quietness, hospitality, friendly disposal and service that will make your vacation in Andros unforgettable. The apartments are constituted by 2 - 3 spaces, with bathroom, kitchen and balcony. All apartments have television, air conditioning, hair-dryer, iron and wireless internet.

Class: Rooms

Tel: +30-22820-22807

Fax: +30-22820-22807

Αρμονια Resort: Hotel "Armonia Resort" is very close to beautiful Chora of Andros island. In a walking distance you will admire the famous Menites springs, the old mansions and the gardens in Lamyra, the fortified houses in medieval Messaria, the museums and the nobility of Chora. Each apartment includes all the amenities for a pleasant stay (large terrace with panoramic view, kitchen, TV, internet connection, central air conditioning, etc).

Class: Hotels

Tel: +30-22820-51000

Fax: +30-22820-51000

Eleni Mansion: Archontiko Eleni (Eleni Mansion) is a 19th Century neoclassical building which adorns the entrance to the market of Chora and combines the neoclassical nobility and the traditional hospitality of the Greek islands with the most modern hotel equipment, offering visitors a convenient and pleasant stay. At the dining room breakfast is served accompanied by home made pastries.

Class: Hotels

Tel: +30-22820-22270

Fax: +30-22820-22294

Vassiliki Studios: Vassiliki Kontou studios are located a few meters from the sandy beach of Chora "Nimporio". 14 A' class one or two rooms apartments, which have separate entrances, are available and include: air conditioning, television, refrigerator, Kitchen, hair dryer, wifi and large balconies. Free parking and a cafe bar by the pool is available.

Class: Rooms

Tel: +30-22820-23547

Fax: +30-22820-25056

Hotel Galini: Hotel Galini has been operating since 1984, offering quality holidays near nature. Built on high ground it has a clear view of the sea which on summer nights with a full moon it becomes so idyllic that it captivates the glance and heart of every visitor. Its amphitheatric position Is noticeably reinforced by the lush green surroundings with trees encircling the hotel all the way down to the sea.

Class: Hotels

Tel: +30-22820-41472

Fax: +30-210-9735069

Elli Appartments: Elli appartments (4 rooms – 3 apartments) is located in Chora of Andros near to the main beach Nimporio (150 meters), in a quiet and calm place with wonderful view to the sea and to the beach! The center of Andros where is the museums , banks, restaurants, walking place etc… is only 150 meters from our place! This appartments are located between the center and the beach of Andros!

Class: Rooms

Tel: +30-22820-22213

Fax: +30-22820-22213

Irene'S Villas: At the beach of Chora (Town), on a verdant hill over the beach of Nimborio are locatedIrene's Villas, little villas recently renovated. The sea is only a few metres away and the view from this hill is astonishing. All villas are fully equipped (kitchen, TV, air-condition, internet, large verandas, parking places).

Class: Rooms

Tel: +30-22820-23344

Fax: +30-22820-24554

Iro Suites: Iro Suites are located at Chora, just one kilometer from the main street with the museums and Niborio beach. Rooms and suites of 16, 22, 34, 44 meters are available. We offer: refrigerator, TV set, air condition, a comfortable bathroom, hair dryer, free wifi, daily service. In 44 meters suites we offer also a fully equipped kitchen and a living room.

Class: Hotels

Tel: +30-22820-25150

Fax: +30-22820-23409

Kalimera Studios: Kalimera Studios are located in the beginning of Chora Town, Andros, on the central road, near the beaches Gialia - Piso Gialia and the beaches of

Chora Nimporio - Paraporti. Kalimera Studios offer satellite TV, fully equipment kitchen, air-condition, central heating, safe, iron - ironing board, daily cleanness of the rooms, hairdryer in the bathroom, free wifi internet, parking.

Class: Rooms

Tel: +30-22820-24382

Fax: +30-22820-24381

Karaoulanis Rooms: Our rooms is located in Chora of Andros near to the main beach Nimporio (150 meters), in a quiet and calm place. The center of Andros where is the museums, banks, restaurants, etc is only 150 meters far away. Our apartments are between 30 and 40 square meters and includes two rooms (with air condition, tv, oven, electric cooker, toaster, coffee machine, hood and fridge) and a bathroom.

Class: Rooms

Tel: +30-22820-22078

Fax: +30-22820-22078

Mainades Maisonettes: Mainades Maisonettes & Studios are two-storey guesthouses for 2-4 persons and four studios, that give another choice to the visitor, who will choose this house complex for his staying. We offer you parking, airconditioning, tv, dvd player, wifi, kitchen, refrigerator, ingredients for a basic breakfast. Daily cleaning services, BBQ.

Class: Hotels

Tel: +30-22820-51888

Fax: +30-22820-51888

Micra Anglia: This chic and stylish 5* hotel deserves its name...A name inspired by the past and glorious epoch of the island of Andros. At Micra Anglia boutique hotel, the glorious past meets with the elegant present day, harmoniously offering ounces of liberty style through an abstract angle which is bound to relax the guest.

Class: Hotels

Tel: +30-22820-22207

Fax: +30-22820-22214

Myrto Studios: In Chora of Andros we created for you, with love Myrto Appartments Group. A little family Hotel settled at a hill just above the main coast of Chora "Neimborio". We offer all the contemporary facilities, suitable for 2-4 persons for unforgettable vacations! Our big garden, the barbeque and a little church make our place the ideal destination to relax and rest.

Class: Rooms

Tel: +30-22820-23673

Fax: +30-22820-23939

Hotel Νικι: The traditional Hotel Niki iw located in the heart of the Andros Island, the pedestrian of Chora, a few meters away from Kairi Square and the museums of Modern Art, Archaeology and Navy. Open all year round and has 6 rooms on the first floor feature 16 beds. All rooms have air conditioning, heating, refrigerator, TV, telephone, safe, WiFi.

Class: Hotels

Tel: +30-22820-29155

Fax: +30-22820-29155

Pansion Moscha: Pansion Moscha is located at the beautiful village of Koumani, just 3 klm off Chora. It comprises of 3 fully equipped apartments (a studio, an one-bedroom apartment and a two-bedroom apartment) which can accommodate from 3 persons to whole families. All apartments of Pansion Moscha are equipped with air-conditioning, heating, fully equipped kitchen, wi-fi, television and parking.

Class: Rooms

Tel: +30-22820-22391

Fax: +30-22820-22391

Paradise Hotel: The elegant balconies of the Paradise Hotel look out onto some of the most magnificent scenery in Greece. A short walk from the hotel brings you to two superb beaches, and all the amenities of Hora. Taverns, cafes, bars and clubs are all easily accessible from the picturesque main street, as are the island's famous museums.

Class: Hotels

Tel: +30-22820-22187

Fax: +30-22820-22340

Hotel Pighi Sariza: Hotel Pighi Sariza located next to the homonymous spring, in the center of Apoikia village. On the first floor is the reception, 6 guests rooms, the fireplace, bar, cafeteria, and the restaurant. All of them have view on a green valley, where on the bottom visitors can see the Aegean sea. We are offering sauna, playroom, billiards and ping-pong.

Class: Hotels

Tel: +30-22820-23799

Fax: +30-22820-22476

Roula Studios: Located at the district of ANEMOMILOI, wich is a 5 minute walk to the pedestrian walkway of HORA Andros, STUDIO ROULA anticipates to accomodate you at a family environment. We offer furnished apartments with 2 to 4 beds, equipped with electric cooker, refrigerator, air condition, led TV, wifi vdsl.

Class: Rooms

Tel: +30-22820-24260

Fax: +30-22820-25140

Saint Louis Studios: SAINT LOUIS welcome you to a relaxed peaceful atmosphere. The ten studio apartments are built in the capital of Andros Chora according to the island style architecture. Studios facilities accommodate max 30 people in ten apartments available with 2, 3 or 4 beds. They include a fully equipped kitchen, electric Kettle, bathroom, T.V, air condition, hairdryer, Wi-Fi available in public areas and a large veranda.

Class: Rooms

Tel: +30-22820-23965

Fax: +30-22820-23928

Sofi′s suites: Located in Chora of Andros, Sofi's Suites features free WiFi, a garden and sun terrace. Archaeological Museum is only 400 m away. All units are air conditioned and feature a flat-screen TV. There is also a kitchenette, equipped with an oven, toaster and refrigerator. A stovetop and coffee machine are also provided. The property also offers packed lunches.

Class: Rooms

Tel: +30-22820-22724

Stylianou Guesthouse: Stylianou guesthouse is located at Nimporio beach, in Chora of Andros. The center of town where are museums , banks, restaurants, walking place is 1 km away. We offer full equipped rooms, with air condition, tv, refrigerator and balkonies with wonderful view to the Aegean sea and Chora. Free wi-fi.

Class: Rooms

Tel: +30-22820-22945

Fax: +30-22820-22945

Faros Studios: We are a small hotel in the beautiful Hora of Andros, beside the sea. Our hotel has four rooms, that can offer hospitality to two to six persons. We provide a little stove, fridge, coffee maker, hairdryer, Iron, a/c, tv, veranda and above all geniality and cordiality.

Class: Rooms

Tel: +30-22820-22762

Fax: +30-22820-22762

Hotels - Rooms Korthi

Korthi Area

Augustis Suites: The newly built complex Augustis Suites is located in the Cyclades island of Andros, in the picturesque coastal town Korthi, 15m. away from crystal beach «Milos». It consists of 10 independent, spacious, luxury apartments for 2-5 people. All have private bathroom, fully equipped kitchen, large balconies with panoramic view, satellite TV, internet, telephone, air conditioning and full service.

Class: Rooms

Tel: +30-22820-61450

Fax: +30-22820-611330

Akrogiali: Akrogiali is located in the center of Korthi Bay. All the apartments have 2 rooms with a view to the sea and their own balcony. Akrogiali has six apartments all equipped with three single beds and an extra sofa bed. The apartments have also heating, air conditioning, refrigerator, fully equipped kitchenette, mini stove, hairdryer, free wi-fi, parking, playing ground for the kids.

Class: Rooms

Tel: +30-22820-61049

Fax: +30-22820-61049

Ammos: Built on an old fig orchard, steps from Milos beach in Ormos Korthiou, Ammos is comprised of 3 double rooms and 2 apartments. The local architecture, the use of natural materials and the landscaping of the grounds harmoniously blend in with the natural environment. Facilities: Full equipped kitchen, air condition, refrigerator, LCD television, safe box, free wifi, hair dryer, iron.

Class: Rooms

Tel: +30-22820-61565

Fax: +30-22820-61565

Villa Mina: Villa Mina is located on the left side of Korthi Bay. The four beds apartments have 2 rooms with view to the sea and their own balcony. The apartments have also heating, air conditioning, refrigerator, fully equipped kitchenette, mini stove, hairdryer, free wi-fi and parking.

Class: Rooms

Tel: +30-22820-61049

Fax: +30-22820-61049

Nicolas Hotel: A brand new world, meticulous to the last detail, waiting for you to experience unique moments of comfort, refined taste and high quality services. On the island of Andros, in a great location near the sea, Nicolas Hotel will become your favorite destination, whatever your desire, a brief escape from everyday life that stands out for its aesthetics and its special color.

Class: Rooms

Tel: +30-22820-61595

Fax: +30-22820-62160

Hotel Korthi: Our family hotel is located on the south coast of Andros, the northernmost island of the Cyclades, on Korthi bay. It is right by the clear blue sea, at the beautiful Korthi beach "Mylos". Our hotel has a total of fifteen (15) rooms, divided into single and double (extra bed can be added upon request).

Class: Hotels

Tel: +30-22820-61218

Fax: +30-22820-61218

Camping

Camping Andros is located in Andros island which is the second largest island of Cyclades. andros campingCamping Andros, amid an olive grove, is located 400 meters from the port of Andros, Gavrio town and 500 meters from the nearest beach. The campsite provides many facilities that will make your vacations very comfortable. It operates from May 1st to September 30th every year and has total of 68 individual pitches to accommodate your tent or caravan and ensure your personal space during your stay.

Location: Gavrion, 84501, Andros island, Greece

Tel: +30 22820 71444 & +30 22820 71044

Monasteries

On the island of Andros you can visit significant monasteries dating from the Byzantine period to the last years of the Ottoman Empire. Some of them have been recently renovated. All of them are of exceptional interest, as they preserve important relics.

The island is rich in religious history, featuring some excellent hagiographers, whose works have been preserved and now decorate various churches on the island. Besides the monasteries, one can also visit old Byzantine churches, such as Taxiarches in Messaria, Melida, Ypsilou, Kimisis Theotokou in Mesathouri and Agios Nikolaos in Korthi. Patron saint of the island is Panagia Theoskepasti church, located in Chora, near "Paraporti" beach. It is celebrated every year on the date of the Akathist Hymn ("Unseated Hymn").

Zoodochos Pigi (Life-Giving Spring) Monastery

It is the largest monastery in Andros. Locals also call it "Agias" and its celebration day is the first Friday after Greek Orthodox Easter Sunday. The date of its construction remains unknown. According to the tradition was used as a school and became a monastery in 842. It hosts rare icons of the 14th and 16th century, a rich library with books and manuscripts, as well as a museum with holy vessels and vestments. There is also a small collection of prehistoric tools. The monastery is officially recorded for the first time in 1400, while the chapel contains an icon dated from 1325. In 1928 the monastery was converted into a convent.

Location: Between Gavrio and Batsi.

How to get there: Following the road from Gavrio to Batsi, after Kypri beach and just before Agios Kyprianos, turn left and follow the uphill road that takes you to the monastery. The distance from Gavrio and Batsi is 7 km, while from Chora 33 km.

Contact Info: (+30) 22820 72459

Panachrantou Monastery

Panachrantou Monastery is located on the slope of Mount Gerakones and is the most beautiful Byzantine monastery of Andros. According to the tradition, it was built by the Emperor Nicephorus II Phocas (963-969), upon his return from the victorious campaign against the Arabs in Crete. The monastery houses the miraculous icon of Virgin Mary, rendered by St Luke. This monastery also possesses the relic skull of St. Panteleimon, which was transferred there from Constantinople in 1705. In Panachrantou Monastery monk "Papoulakos" was imprisoned. The monastery, which was recently renovated, is celebrated on July 27th (St. Panteleimon's day) and on August 15th. Abbot of the monastery is Father Evdokimos Fragoulakis, who serves there since 1957.

Location: Near to Chora and just above Falika village.

How to get there: Following the road from Falika village. Alternatively, you can follow the road from Chora to Korthi and turn towards Vouni village (check relevant road signs). The distance from Chora is 4 km and from Korthi 13 km.

Contact Info: (+30) 22820 51090 - http://impanahrantou.blogspot.gr

Agia Marina (St. Marina) Monastery

Agia Marina's monastery is located north of Chora and was recently renovated. The monastery dates from 1325, when Agia Marina shows herself to an elder monk at Litres region and indicates him to find her icon in a slot of a rock... And so it happened. During the 16th century, the monastery is burned three times from the pirates, but monk Sofronios fully refurbishes it by selling his property in Peloponnese.

He converted it to a convent, hosting up to 100 nuns. In 1833, 417 monasteries in Greece are closing by order, among which Agia Marina. Embirikos family bought the miraculous icon and transfers it to the Church of Virgin Mary in Chora. In 1975, Dorotheos, Metropolitan of Syros, asks Deacon Kyprianos Chimonas to restore the monastery and the latter follow his will. The monastery became widely known by the miraculous healing of a small child from Cyprus.

Location: North of Chora, in a 4 km distance from Apikia region.

How to get there: Follow the road from Chora to Apikia and turn left at the intersection that leads to Ypsilou and Strapourgies villages. Then take the road on your right towards the monastery. There are relevant road signs.

Contact Info: (+30) 22820 24074

Agios Nikolaos (St. Nicholas) Monastery

Agios Nikolaos monastery, with its an elaborate architectural structure, is perfectly maintained. According to tradition, the monastery was built during the 11th century, while in 1760 extensive repairs were made. The monastery is fortified with high walls and the katholikon is cross-in-square type, two-columned with narthex and a dome. There are many chapels inside the monastery. Here are kept the relic skull of Saint Nicholas of Vounenois, the jawbone of St. Kosmas Aitolos, part of the skull of St. Joseph of Arimathea and many other relics. The Monastery was annex of "Filiki Eteria" and served as a printing and bindery house, as well as "Krifo scholio" (Secret School) during the Turkish occupation, due to its outermost location. Monastery's iconostasis is unique and holy water spouts from the altar. The monastery's wooden screen is superb, while there are also traces of frescoes.

Location: North of Apikia and before Vourkoti village, in a 10 km distance from Chora and 25 km from Batsi.

How to get there: Follow the road from Chora to Apikia and turn right after Apikia and before Vourkoti village. There are relevant road signs.

Contact Info: (+30) 22820 22190

Gastronomy

When referring to the gastronomy of Andros, one should first mention its desserts and especially its spoon sweets or preservesmade of fruits and sugar. The most popular ones are the walnut (the island abounds in walnut trees), the bitter orange, the "rose" from rose petals, the sour cherry and the great "lemon flower" sweet. It is also worth tasting the traditional spoon sweet "pampiloni", made from the large aromatic citrus fruit of the island, as well as the bergamot.

Other famous desserts are the "Amygdalota" (made from marzipan and flower water) which have a unique scent and flavor, "Kaltsounia" with nuts and honey filling, and "Pasteli" (sesame seed candy) made of local walnuts and sesame. Therefore "Pastelaries" is a special treat: It is dried figs with ground walnuts, cinnamon and sesame. In the island's pastry shops you can find also "Soumada", a cold drink made of bitter almonds which is usually offered at weddings.

Although there is not an organized distillery on the island, you can easily find (mostly in women associations) homemade liqueurs and raki, like "Potzi", a type of "rakomelo" (mixture of raki and honey). In the past, locals made "Potzi" using berry raki, which is stronger in alcohol. There are several vineyards, but yet not a winery. It is worth drinking the red wine made of "Koumari" (a village) variety of wines.

Andros used to have (and still has) a significant tradition in stock farming and cheese production. Currently, small units are operating in the island, producing high quality cheeses. Here are the most important ones:

Petroti or Armexia or Analati: it is a white fresh cow cheese with a semi-hard texture, particularly tasty and full of flavors. You can eat it plain or with food, make pies or serve it with dried fruits as a dessert.

Volaki: It is made of pasteurised cow's milk. It is cone shaped with rich buttery flavour and a texture similar to mozzarella. You can use it in salads or eat it with just a slice of bread. When left for some time in the refrigerator, it obtains a hard texture, an ochre colour and a spicy flavour, making it an ideal "meze" (snack) for raki. You may also grate it over pasta.

Spicy kopanisti: Made of the Greek cheese "mizithra", when placed in a clay pot and fermented with salt. The kneading process is periodically repeated 3 times. It is pressed very tightly for an airtight result and covered with a cloth soaked in vinegar. It will be ready to serve after ten days.

As for food in general, the island's "trademark" is froutalia. It is an omelette made of potatoes cut into thin round slices, herbs, local sausages and "glyna" (pork fat), which give froutalia its special flavour. There are many variations worth tasting. For example, froutalia with fresh broad beans, zucchini, artichoke or zucchini blossoms.

In Andros, apart from the excellent homemade sausages with the flavour of anise, you can also find "Louzes" - smoked pieces of pork, marinated in red wine also with fennel and pepper.

"Lampriatis" which is an Easter traditional dish, holds a special place in the cuisine of Andros. It is made of lamb stuffed with a mixture of three different types of cheese, eggs, rice, spearmint and parsley, slowly baked in a wood oven for about 8-10 hours

* 9 7 8 9 7 8 5 0 7 6 8 4 4 *